POETRY.PROSE.ART

3:40 a.m.

FROM HEART TO HEAD

Written By
URJA JOSHI

Anecdote
Publishing House
For the love of quality reading!

To *grief*.
For I'd never know,
How to appreciate the joyful days of my life,
Without you.

Dear you,
It's you,
the light that you're searching,
the home that you feel homesick for.

Anecdote Publishing House
2nd Floor 2/15 Lane no. 2 Ansari Road,
Daryaganj-110002

Published by Anecdote Publishing House
Copyright © Urja joshi

First Edition 2024

ISBN 978-81-968952-6-6

MRP ₹ 350

All Rights Reserved.
No part of this publication may be reproduced, stored in a retrieval system, or transmitted in any form, or by any means—electronic, mechanical, photocopying, recording or otherwise—without the prior permission of the publisher. Opinions expressed in it are the author's own. The publisher is in no way responsible for these.

Book Promoted and Marketed by Champ Readers Pvt. Ltd.
Cover design by Sumedha Mahajan
Layout by Graphic Tailor
Printed by Thomson Press (India) Ltd, New Delhi

Contents

Prologue :　　　　　　　　　　　　　　　vii
Who is she?
ZARA

Chapter: heart　　　　　　　　　　　　　　1
(grief)

Chapter: head　　　　　　　　　　　　　　86
(acceptance)

Chapter: soul　　　　　　　　　　　　　　166
(letters from the diary)

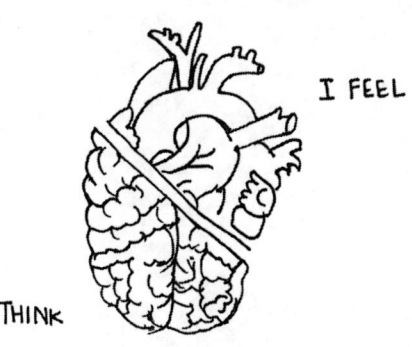

Prologue:
Who is she?

Zara
a woman made out of determination of logic and vulnerability of emotion, she is resilient but she knows when to break, she is the joy but nobody cries better than her. She has the courage to accept, but no one has grieved the way she did.
Zara is a union of logic & emotion, a woman where the innocence of the heart & the judgement of the head meet, a character, who feels like home, a story we all have lived, she is the definition of beginning again after endings, and endings after beginning.
 Zara is a reminder to us that sometimes in our lives the only saviour that will show up for us, is our own self, sometimes the knight in shining armour, isn't a better partner than the last one, or a better job or moving away from your hometown or making new friends to forget about the old ones or a new story, a new name, sometimes it's you.
The you who chose to live despite it all, a version of you who wiped your tears and still showed up for your healing, that version of you is a gift, that version is where all the battles of logic and emotion end, that version is ZARA.

Therapist:
you texted me at 3:40 in the morning
"I feel like I am falling"
Why do you feel that way?

Zara:
Life

chapter: Heart
(grieving)

On some days,
I feel so
All over the place.
I feel like
I am scattered

                  Everywhere

        Like stars

                      In the sky

         And words

                    On this page.

after 10 years, I imagine our meeting to be something like this : you come to me, and ask if I still think about you and then I see myself answering, "you never left my mind
you should be asking
If I ever take rest from thinking about you."

(//if you think time changes feelings)

I spoke
I'd love me,
If I was better.
And my soul laughed
From inside,
Knowing, even if I was the best creation of this universe
I'd still want to be
Someone else.

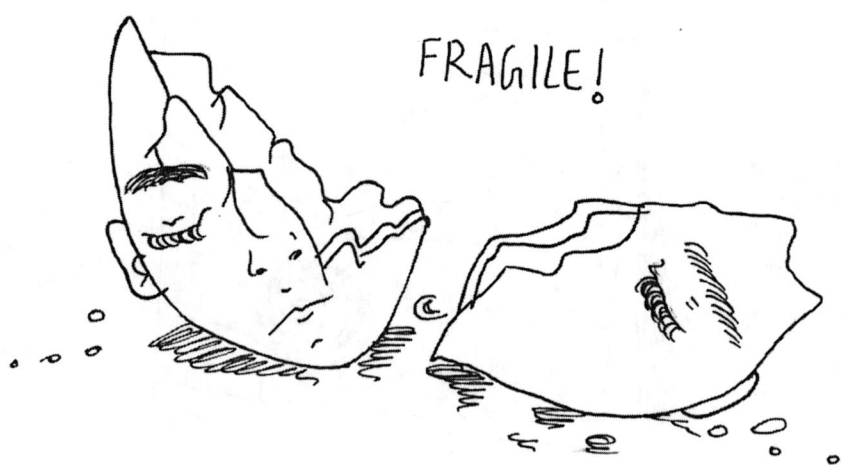

I left
not because
there wasn't enough love
Between us,
But because there was so much love
That I felt
So unloved by myself.
All the love
that I had
I poured it all into you.

(I had none left for me)

3:40 A.M. From heart to head

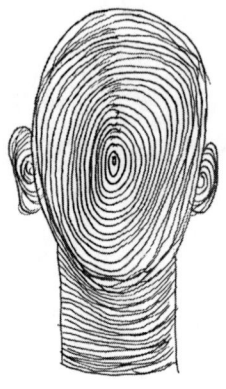 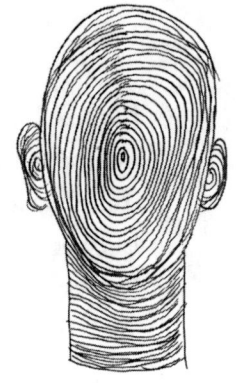

yesterday
Someone told me that
My sadness is not relevant
Because it was
Not as big as depression
And today
I am telling you that
Even if it hits for 5 minutes
I know that it pains.

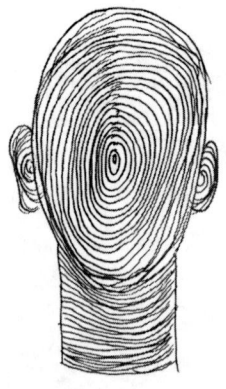 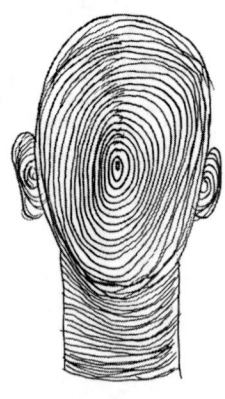

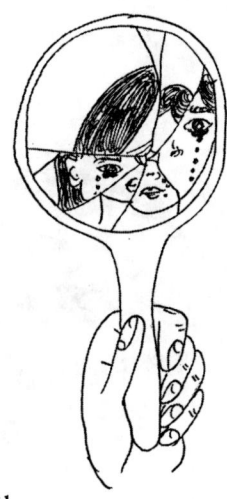

I remember how it was like,
November of last year.
Everyone around me
Wanted me to do my favourite things
So that I can get my mind off you.
But I did not want to.
The world said that it will bring me happiness.
But I remember how it was like,
I wanted happiness to come to me,
Only if you came with it too.

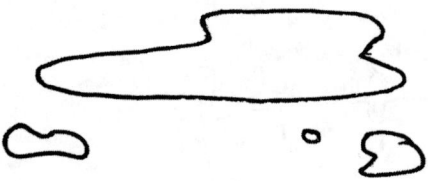

3:40 A.M. From heart to head

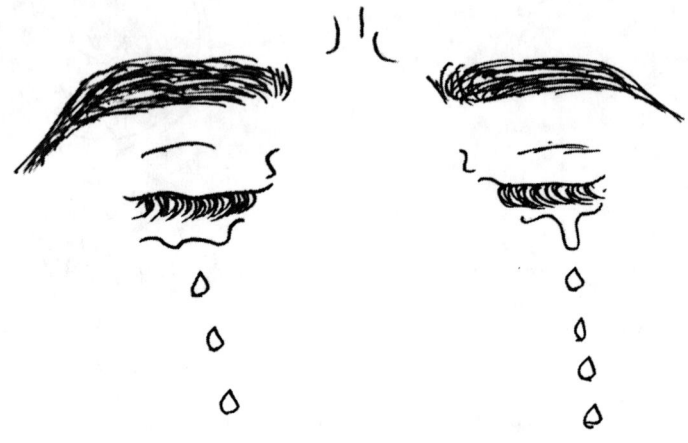

Why are they everywhere,
Even when
they are gone.

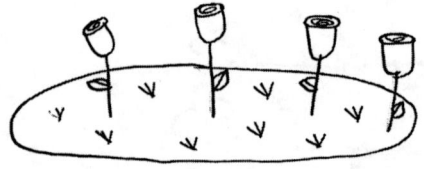

I don't envy
The girls near you,
For they know
Only what you want them to know.
I envy
the walls of your rooms,
Who've seen how you look
At 3 am in morning.
And who've heard every conversation of yours.
Who know when you actually sleep,
After texting goodnight to people, you talk to.
I envy the sun
Which gets to shine
On your skin
And make it gleam.
I envy every phenomenon
Which witnesses you
On days when I've no clue
What you are up to.

  —My kind of jealousy

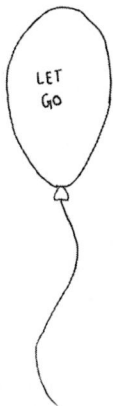

I go to stores
To buy stuff for myself.
But I smile whenever I see your
Favourite ice cream
Or a misspelled word
That I know would make you laugh.
hence it's safe to conclude that
Even when I am alone
Doing nothing but just trying to exist like a normal girl,
Even after knowing that we have parted our ways,
Your thought never leaves me.
I still live my life
Pretending
It has you in it.

—Flashbacks

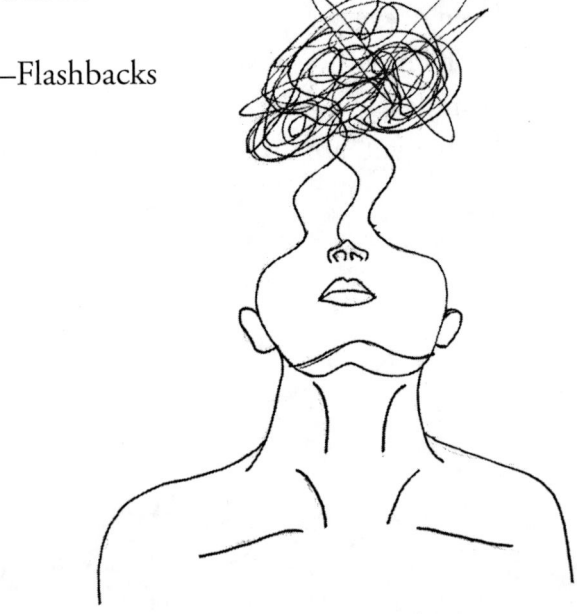

But you always ask me,
If it's possible for me
To love someone else,
let me tell you
How impossible is that,
Who will accept this love
Which has
Your name written all over it.

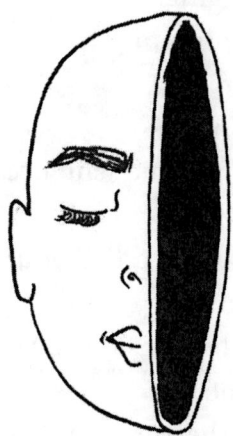 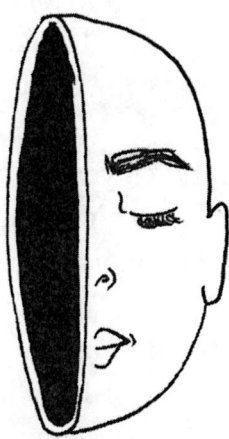

The circle of life,
You beg for it
And then
After some years
Someone else is begging for
The same bare minimum
You once wanted.
You are arguing
And then you are speaking the same sentences
Your parents said to you
The things your abusive partner called you
Over the years
You become the pain that lives inside you,
Breaking someone else
Just because you were broken the same way once.

—The history of grief

(The resistance to go to therapy)

I couldn't convince myself
That I needed someone qualified, to understand my grief.
I wasn't ready to accept that my grief was complex now,
That now ranting and crying wouldn't work.
I wasn't ready to accept that maybe my grief was so much more than just sadness.
I wasn't ready to accept that I needed help of someone else
To understand my own mind,
My own heart,
I stayed far from it, for years.
I was afraid of meeting my past again, in my therapist's cabin,
I was afraid of being misunderstood by someone else,
After being misunderstood by myself.
If I can't trust my own self, with my baggage,
Then how will I trust some other individual with it.

3:40 A.M. From heart to head

It was not even
love in the first place.
If they claimed
to love you
before sleeping,
and then tried to
change everything about you
the next morning.

[acceptance is another name for love]

They congratulate me
for finally leaving you behind
and moving forward in life.
When only I know
That I still look
For you in everyone I meet.
I look for the shine of your eyes
In every pair of eyes, I have stared back in.
I look for the warmth of your hand,
When I hold hands with someone new.
I hug everybody to see,
If I will ever feel the way,
I felt when we hugged.
Have I really left you behind
If I am still searching for the idea of you,
In a new human.

3:40 A.M. From heart to head

Sometimes,
you spend
so many years of your life
looking
for a safe pair of hands.
Which will hold yours
and understand
exactly what you've been through
And wont dare to hurt you
Like that again.

(someone who gets how tired you are.)

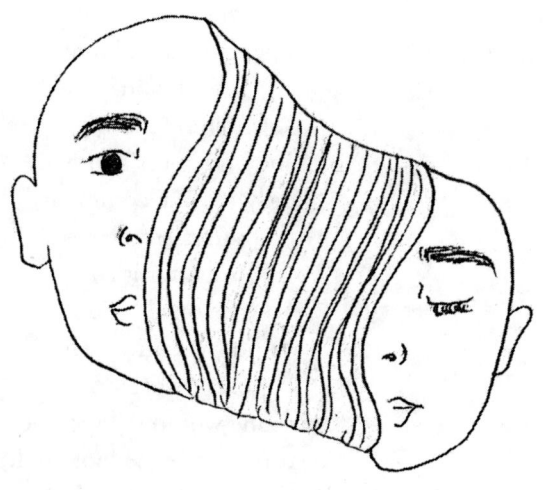

How is it possible
That
I've lived with myself
For a lifetime
And I think
It's me, who I know the least.

[Time spent together
Can never predict
How much people know each other.]

3:40 A.M. From heart to head

For me,
Self confidence
Was this huge
Fragile, brick wall.
I spent years building it
Bit by bit
Carefully placing
One brick over another.
Only for one comment
From a stranger
To shatter it all.
One conversation
And the entire wall
Loses its balance.
Someone would tell me once
That red made me look dull,
And I'd never shop for red clothes again,
Despite of how happy it made me.
For me
Self confidence
Was this huge fragile brick wall
And I hope
One day I am able to hold it together
No matter how strong
The winds of criticism are.
No matter how loud the voices are.

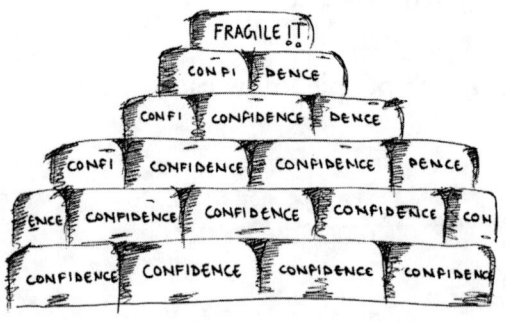

If you ever forget about yourself
And ask yourself
Who are you?
You are the Silence
in between of my words.
You are the peace before the storm
& You are, what is left
After the war.
You are the comfort of the weekends
And chaos of late nights
You are the thought that I overthink
Yet you are the only one
Who I think of, when I need to be calmed.
You are the one
I am thankful for
Yet on some days
 you remain the one
Who I regret having the most.

When you walk into heartbreak again
You hope
To know it better than before
You say to yourself
I have been here before
Then
Why do I still
Don't know
What to do.
Years of living this way
And I still haven't perfected
The way I handle sadness
On some days.

[I hope you say
I have been here before
I know this feeling
This time
I know
What to do]

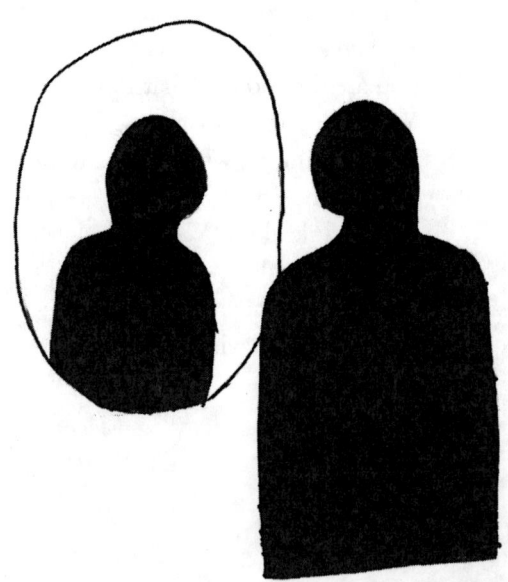

The air leaving your lungs,
The blood rush,
The different feelings,
Travelling
From your heart to head,
And the process of your head
Trying to make sense out of it.
You feel all of it
& Every bit of it
When anxiety happens.

Some decisions
Will make sense to your head,
But will leave your heart
Aching for the rest of your life.

-       Logic and emotion

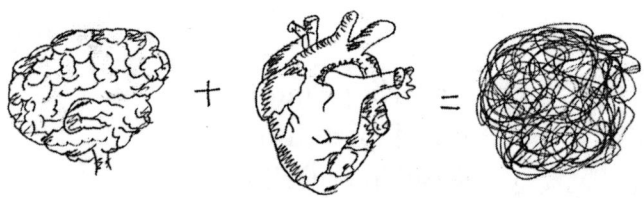

I want to trust myself
I want to believe
When people say they love me
I want to believe
When people say they think I am amazing
I want to believe
When people say they think I am beautiful
I want to end these conflicts
Going in my head
I want to believe everything
And not these voices in my head
Which convince me
I am nothing like what they all say.

(overthinking)

3:40 A.M. From heart to head

Questions at 3:40 a.m.

Am I okay?/no I'm thinking too much/its temporary/does everyone feel this way/will I ever feel like myself again/no I'm thinking too much/does it get better/what if it gets worse/will I feel different if I move away from home/what if this feeling meets me again there/am I unstable/I think I should call them/maybe ending the life will make it better/no I'm thinking too much/should I call mother/she'll never understand/should I call dad/what if he thinks I am too weak/do I even matter/
They leave no matter what/I think it's me/I am the cause of every problem/I can't take it anymore/this is too heavy to carry/or am I just too weak/

No I'm thinking too much

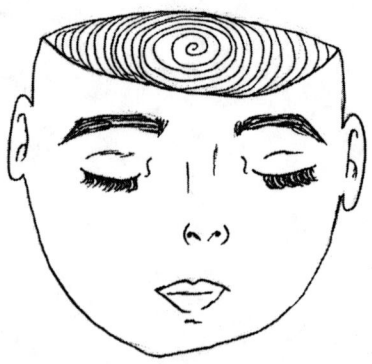

Every time you push me away,
It becomes harder
To come back.
So when you walk out the doors of my heart
Remember
I am not longing for you anymore,
I am growing
Used to your absence.
You are teaching me
To live without you.

If I could get
A minute
With you again,
All I'd do
Is ask you
If you're proud of me
And I know,
You will say you are,
I know you always were.
Your faith in me
Was the starting of me having faith in myself.
I need you to come here
And remind me of my greatness once again.

— Grandpa, 7th march 2018
    Mizpah: (n.) the deep emotional bond between people, especially separated by distance or death.

Am I kind
If I am kind to this whole world
But not to me.

Am I loving
If I can give my love
To everyone
Except myself.

Am I really accepting
If it takes a minute for me
To accept other's flaws
But forever
To accept my own.
Am I beautiful
If I only believe in it
When others say that to me.

Am I an artist
If my art
Is only significant to me
When others validate that for me

Am I
Who I think I am
If my whole life
Is completed
By what others do to me.

There was a time
When my heart was so alive
That I could feel
Emotions of every person who touched my hand.
I thought about what it's like to harden up so much
That a tear from your eye feels like a miracle.
but now that I have muted it
Now that my head has come to life
To make sense out of every breathe I take
I want the heart back.
I want my insides to soften again
I want to feel everything once again.

(the aftermath of loss)

There were days
When nothing would shake me.
The kind of unusual strength
Like the world could end but I knew
I'll be just fine
And I have lived some days
Where they'd ask
"How are you?"
And I was already spilling through my eyes.

(my extreme ends)

Home was you,
The first place
Where I felt belonged.
The first place
I wanted to run from,
Just to see
If the place I called home
Would be homesick
For mee too.

[I had only one question on my mind
For years,
Do you want me
The way I want you.]

I wanted you to stay
So I held on to you,
So tight,
Thinking you won't slip now,
But the tighter I wrapped my hand around you,
The more you wanted to slip away.

[Let it go / slipped away like sand of the beach]

Even when I wanted to be alone,
I hoped that
You'd somehow find me
In my loneliness.
And speak
That you don't have to be this way
When I am here.
& You would think I want you to get me the world
But all I have ever wanted
Is just you to care enough.

(is it too much to ask for)

I felt numb for so long,
I did not cry over anything for months,
I'd feel something is wrong with the way my heart feels.
And today I broke down,
Because I forgot to order
My food correctly.
I cried over how I can't get even this straight,
And I realized,
The small things become so big,
When you spend your days pretending
That the big things are small.
Your grief will find an exit
In so many little ways
Because you don't let your heart grieve
The way it deserves to.

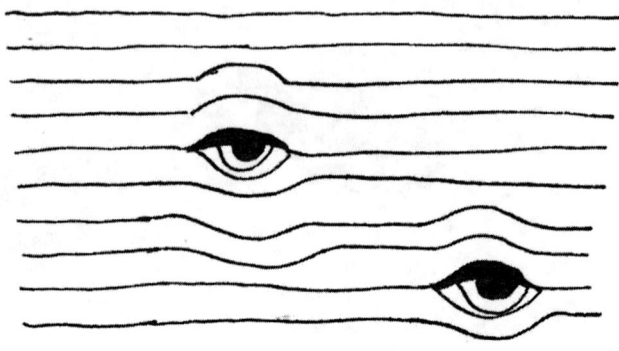

There was
So much of yesterday in me
That living in today
Felt like a punishment.
I either wanted to run back in time
Where everything was alright and untouched
Or to the future
So far in time
Where I have forgotten
Everything bad that ever made me feel anything.

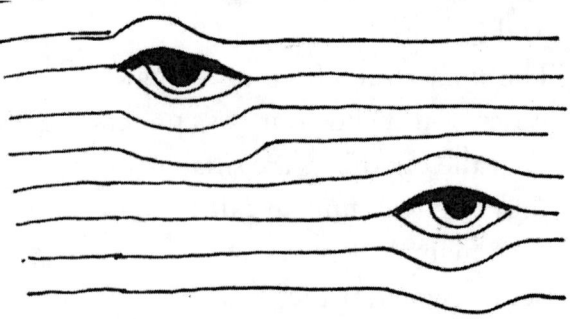

Urja Joshi

I don't know how
I loved so fiercely
I gave you
All of me
I called me yours
And after your leaving
I don't know
What to call me
I wake up
In the morning
Trying to remember
My identity
Who am I,
without you?

-co dependency

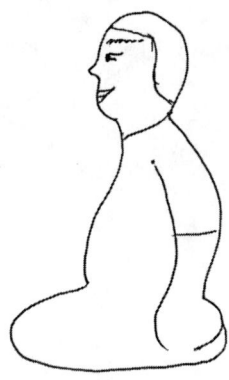

3:40 A.M. From heart to head

I expected a different ending,
From same stories.
I expected,
Someone to treat me differently,
While I remained the same.
I walked down the same roads,
Knocked the same doors,
And wanted someone else
To open those doors.
Forgetting that no matter what I do,
The pain will remain the same,
If I am the same.
That change starts
From within,
And not by changing the
People, I find home in.

We're okay

                    No we're not, I feel the pain

No we're fine
It happens to
Everyone

                    Yes but I want to talk to someone

They'll think
We're weak

                              But
                              We're lonely

Only strong people
Are alone

                        Is it worth it
                        Being lonely
                      & having so much strength

Its better then
Being walked upon

                  But no one will ever check up on us
                      If we won't ask for help

No one did
Even when we did

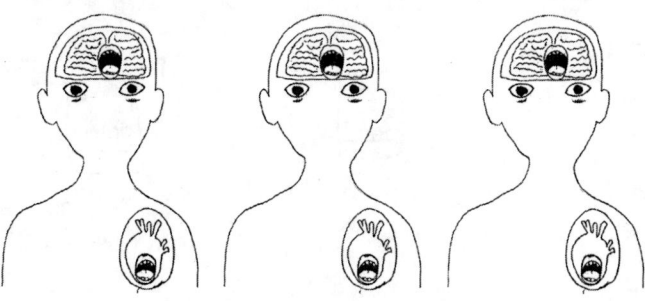

They always leave mentally,
Before
They take their body with them.
For you
It was just one random day,
When they decided to go.
But for them
It has been months and years
Of preparing.
two people
In the same relationship ,
Experiencing the same separation
So differently.

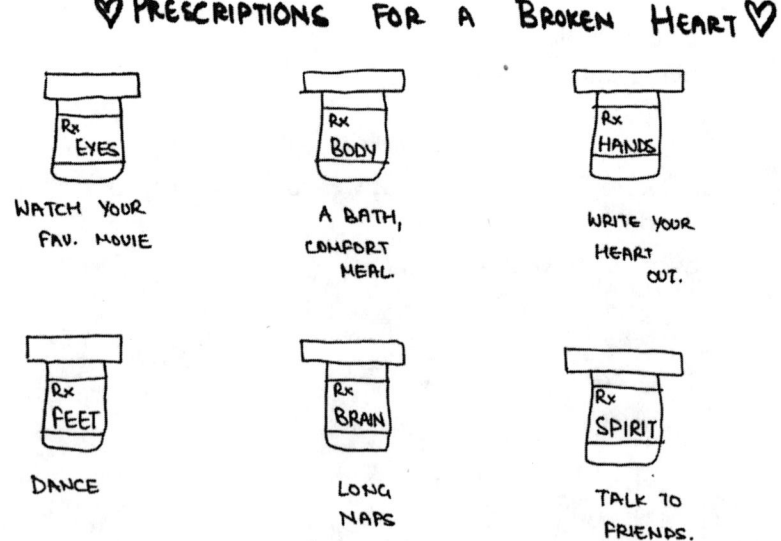

And no one
Talks about
All the effort
That goes
in forgetting something
Which was
All that you wanted
To remember.

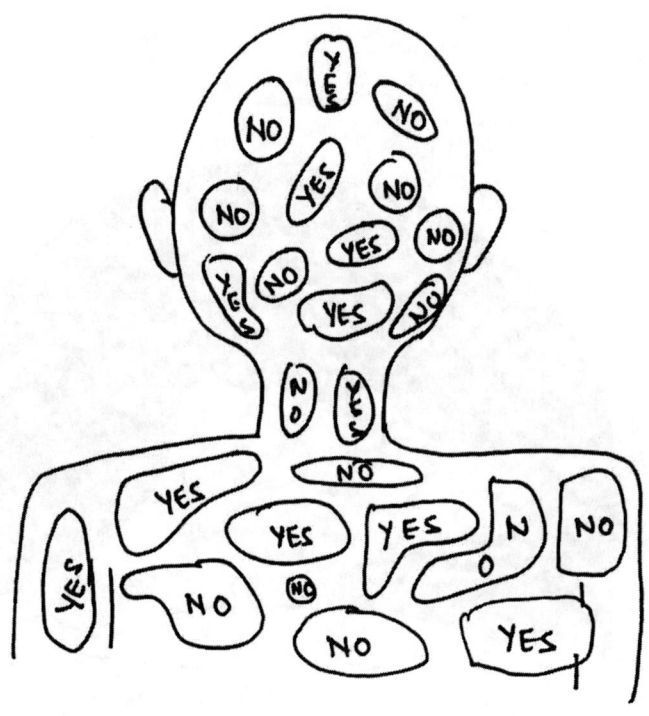

3:40 A.M. From heart to head

They complain
And throw things at you
Because of what you've become
Not realizing
They made you
What they hate now.

(everything that I learnt from you, became
Everything you couldn't take.)

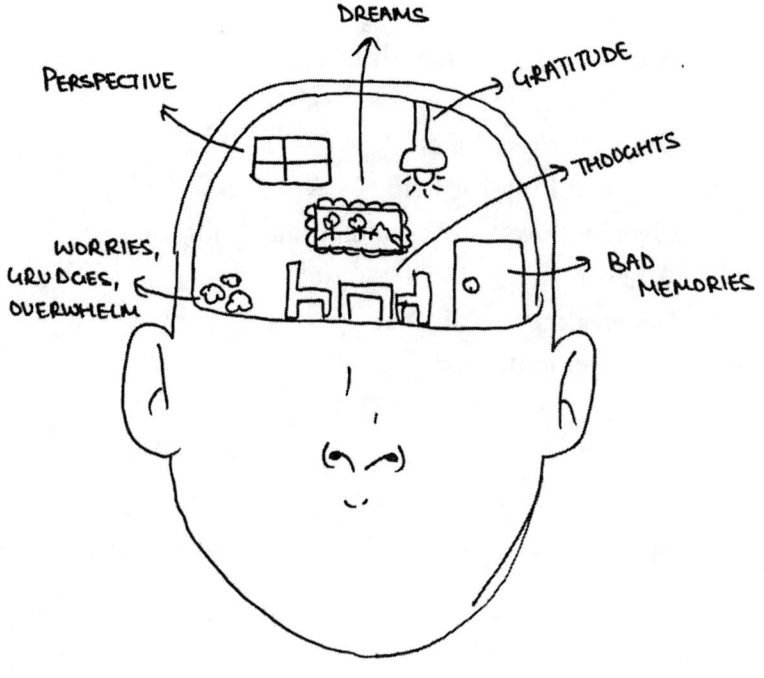

I live
inside my head so much that
I can rarely listen to my heart beating.
I approach everything in life
With logic so often
That now emotions
Feel like a weakness.

(disassociation)

I don't open up
About my grief,
About my hopelessness,
Because what if they think
That's all I am.
What if my sadness
Or me asking for help
Overshadows every good thing about me
What if
My weakness is all that
 I am remembered for.

   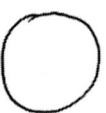

ANGER　　　　JOY　　　　ANXIETY　　　　DEPRESSION

I am sorry
That I search for
Everything that is missing,
In you.
That must be a lot to take
My 9 year old self
Searches for the emotional
Intimacy, in you.
That she did not find anywhere else
My 14-year-old trauma searches that validation
In you.
My 19 year old woman
Searches for meanings of love inside you.
It must be a lot to take
I am sorry
That I love you
With everything in me.
My bad past
My hopeful future
My nonexistent present.
I am sorry
For putting you through my love
When this should've been
The most euphoric experience of your life.

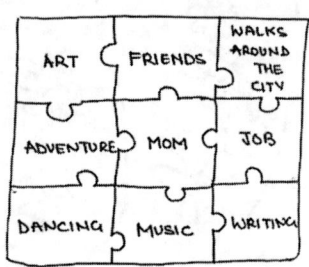

You've been through so much
That now your eyes get welled up
And voice breaks
When someone asks
If you are really happy.
As if the question has summoned every voice in your head
"no I am not, no I am not, no I am not"
But you always say, you're alright
Because your 3 am overthinking has convinced you
That no one will ever get you.
But on some days
You don't have to say what's on your mind
To be understood,
You can say it
because it's too heavy to carry forever.

(I wish I talked about it more)

You want so much from life
When you're a kid
You want the big things
You want the best of every thing
But then something happens
Someone walks in
And takes out so much meaning
Out of your life
That now
You just want to be happier
Than the day before.

(I want big things from life again)

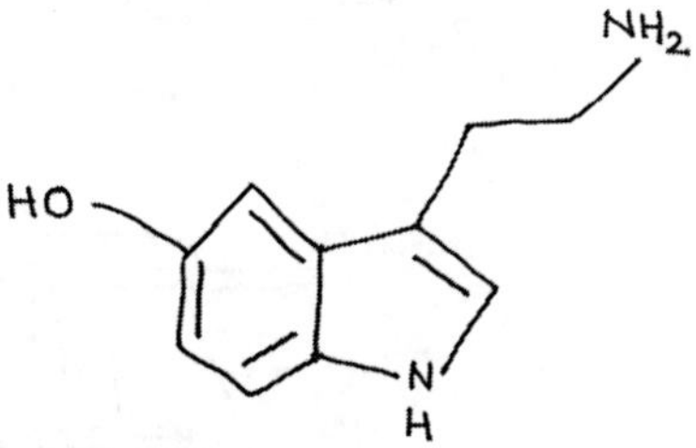

Serotonin
(Happiness)

3:40 A.M. From heart to head

I know
That you live in this world
But you wish
You belonged here more.
You wish it felt
More like home.

I was put in a room,
With everything and everyone
I have loved dearly in my life.
And I remember
I walked up to you
And said
"You shouldn't be here
I have loved everything else in this room
But what I had for you
Was so much more than that,
I am forever changed
By what you did
And how you left
You don't deserve to be here
Because you're the only thing
I wish wasn't here
Only thing I want to forget about."

3:40 A.M. From heart to head

When you sit in front of me
I want to have both your body and mind
Right here
In this room,
In the same place as you.
Because what will I do
With a person
Who talks to me
But thinks of someone else
What's the point
Of me being here with you,
In your present .
But not being anywhere
When you talk about the future.

My life is good
Without you.
But I won't deny
That it
Would have been better
If you were here.

[a little less alone]

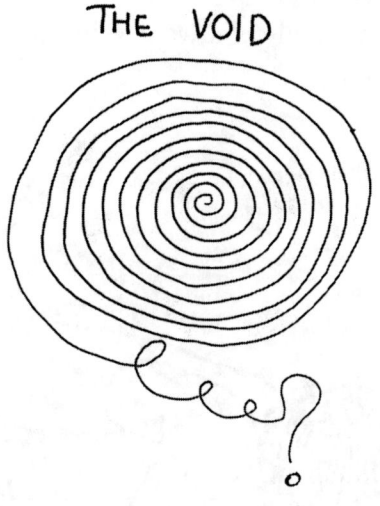

3:40 A.M. From heart to head

In another universe
I know exactly what to do
With a broken heart.
I know what to say
When they ask me where do I see myself in a decade.
I know how to take compliments.
I know how to clap for others without feeling,
I am what is left behind.
In another universe,
I know when to walk away.
I know how to be in love with myself.
I wake up every day,
And tell myself,
That in another universe,
I am living the way
I could have,
I am a human, who I always wanted to be,
In some reality.

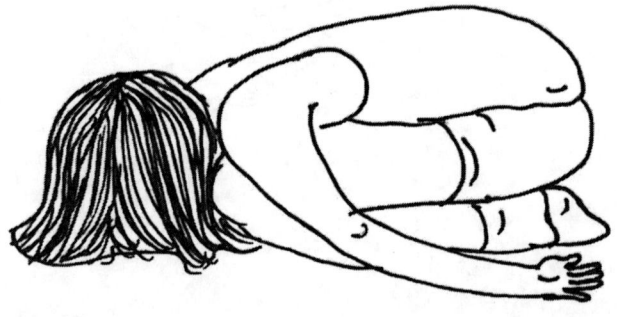

I waited so long
To be loved by you.
I got so desperate ,
That your little words,
Would make me wonder
If you finally love me,
Even for a few seconds
The way I have loved you
For Every day of my life.
Your mood would become my mood,
Your bad day would mean my worst day,
If you say something nice,
I would feel like I have made it as a human.
And when you did not,
I would feel like the biggest failure.
I'd change so much about me,
My hair, my clothes, my voice
Only for you to not notice anything.
I left so much of me behind,
Because I was busy chasing you.
I felt away from you even when we were in the same room.
But what would be worse than
Me feeling so away from my own self
Even when I was living in this body.

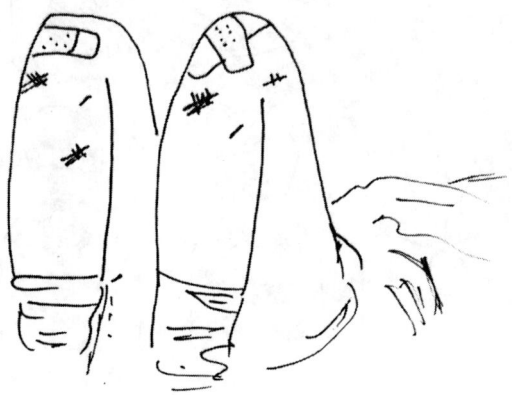

3:40 A.M. From heart to head

I was so afraid of the world
Seeing me
For who I truly am
What if
Everything that I am
Was everything they did not want.

[my different seasons]

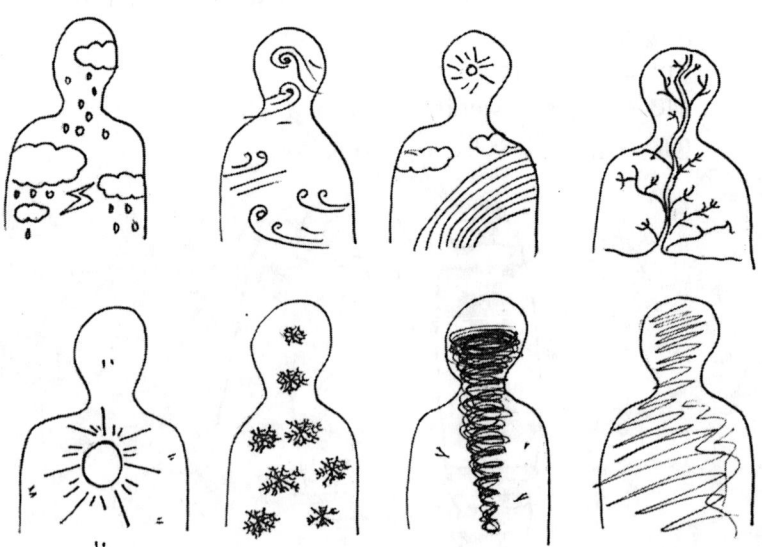

When I was young,
I thought grief was what we feel
When someone leaves us
Without any warning.
But as I progressed in age
I realized that grief had a different spelling
For everyone.
For some it was having everything yet waking up with an empty feeling in chest.
For some it was leaving behind their hometown
 to pursue their dreams in another city.
For some it was not speaking to their best friend anymore
For some it was losing a child.
For some it was having heavy regrets about past
For some it was the struggle to open up to their own father.
For some it was watching their parents' marriage fail,
For some it was shattering of a dream.
Grief is nothing but leaving & loss
But what we leave & lose
Is different for each one of us. .
We are a world of 8 billion people
With 8 billion different reasons to grieve.
You can't compare the heaviness of what you're carrying with some other person.

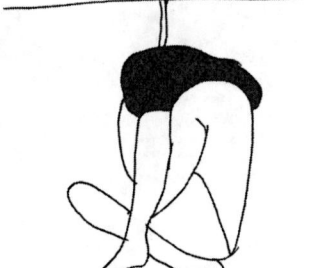

3:40 A.M. From heart to head

They did not know how to love you
And now
You don't know
What to do with someone
Who actually does.

(You forget how to flow like that once again for someone else)

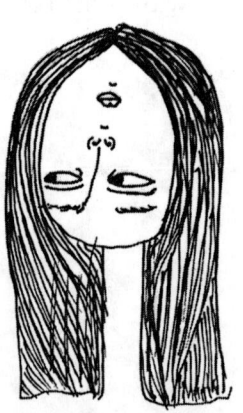

I've never heard him say
I love you
But his love is the only love
That I trust blindly.
a knowing with certainty
that he will be there
when even God turns his back to me.

(Sometimes we seek words
when what they give us,
is a love greater than that)

I was so naïve
To think that happiness and love
Have to coexist.
You can be so in love
Yet so unhappy
At the same time.
If you're not chosen
The way
You choose them.
If you don't affect their existence
The way
They affect yours.

[When you love the wrong one]

I know
What it means
To be in love with someone,
And to have them,
It's rare,
And it's a blessing.
Because I also know
What it takes
To walk out of something
You thought
You'd have till you die.
You thought was only yours
I know what it takes
To pack it up
And leave a little earlier than forever.
And this thought alone
That now you will spend your life
With anyone but them,
Everyone but them,
That there is stranger
That exists, who knows
You better than you.
Wrecks your soul.

3:40 A.M. From heart to head

Days go by
When I don't live in my body,
Days go by
When I live inside my head.
I can rarely listen to my heart beating
& I have left so many days, months & years
Behind me
Without me having a significant memory.
Because I am everywhere
But right here
In this moment.

If you ever ask me what is the right time to let go of someone? I will always say that the moment it all starts messing with you, the moment you start feeling unsure about
where exactly you stand, the moment you start thinking, if you are even a part of their thought, when they are on your mind every day. If you are even someone's second or third or fourth choice. When you will choose them over this entire world any day.
I think that's the exact moment you walk out. If anything is meant to be yours there will never be questions, there will be no confusions & no waiting for them to treat you right.

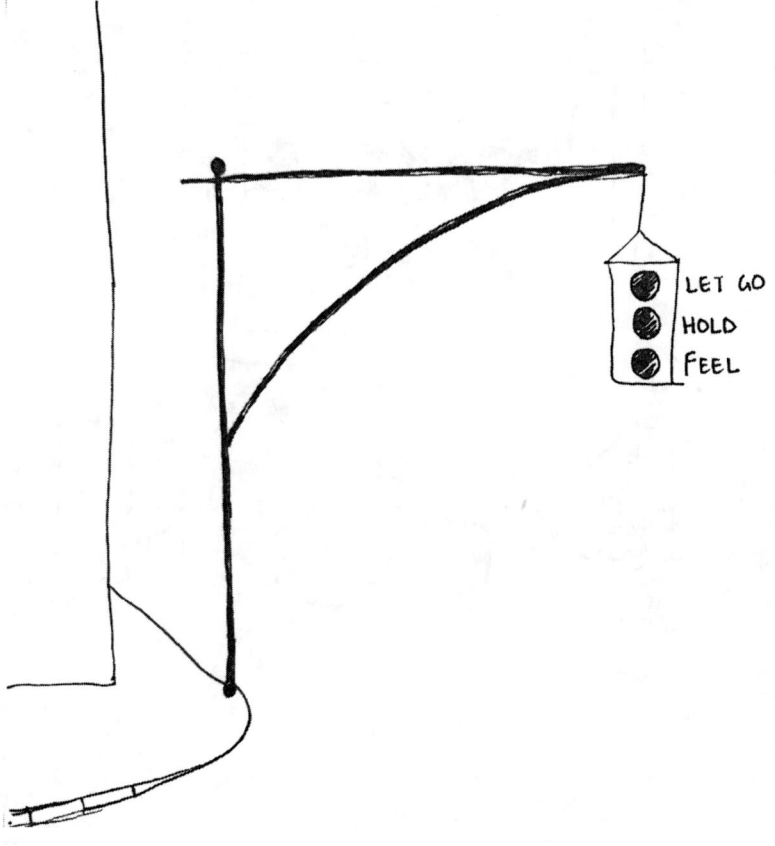

"I have been working since I was 14
I love what I do
But mom
Am I wrong to be tired of something that
makes me so happy
I want a break
I want to love me, the way I love my work."

- Burnout

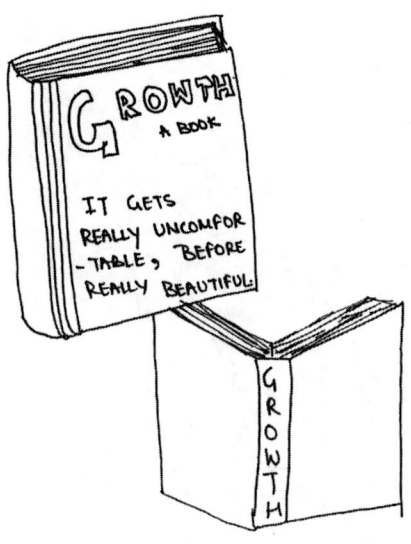

Growth
Was always happening
When I was 14
When I turned 19
When I will be 30
Am I always supposed to
Leave behind my old selves
And transform into a new human.
When does it stop
What is the final version of me
I am tired of breaking & building
Myself, again and again
Can I stop and enjoy living for 3 minutes.

(what will I tell them, when they ask me,
how was life, after my death)

3:40 A.M. From heart to head

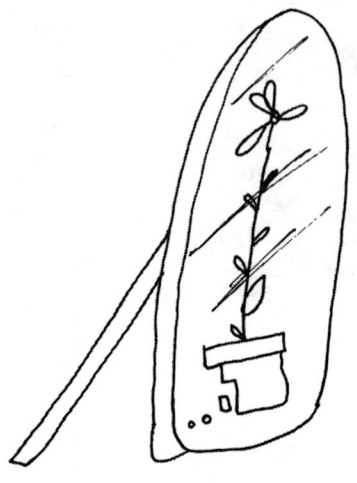

You were sitting
In front of me
And I was
Missing those parts of you
Which already left
A long time ago.
The part of you, that cared enough
The part of you, that was loving
The part of you, which remembered
That I don't like when you don't make conversations.
You were sitting
In front of me
And I was
Watching you become a new version
Of yourself.
Someone, I was scared, you'll become eventually.

I walked into chaos
And it welcomed me.
Asking me
Are you alone?
Where are they
Who made promises of being there for you always.
I had nothing to say
Chaos made me realize
I am all that I've got
Till the very end.
It made me realize
That I can have an army of 100 people
Around me
But when I'll have to go to war with myself
It will only be me
& no one else.

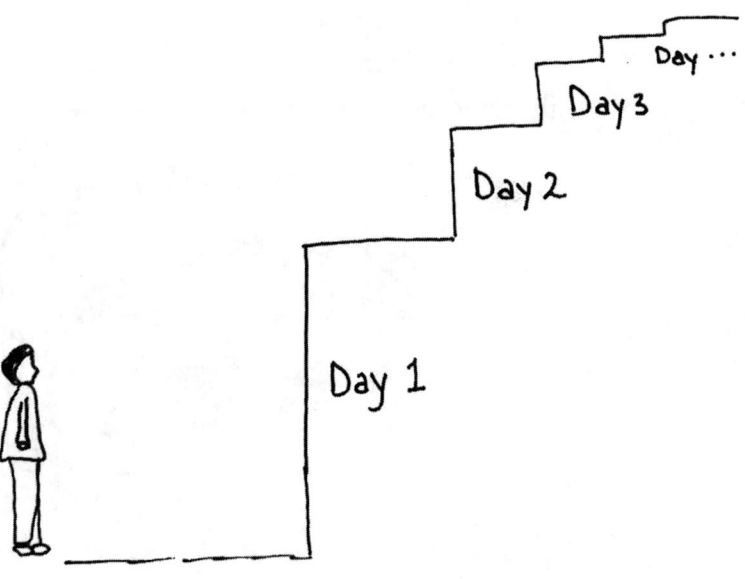

Sorrow visits me
At 3 am
With your memories in her hand.
Asking "do you remember?"
And I smile, replying
"of course, I do"
How can I forget one thing
That made me feel both
The most alive and dead inside at the same time.

Your body is your home
Your museum
Yet
You let people
Walk in you
And decide
What paintings aren't good enough for your walls,
What colour doesn't look good on you.
Why do they get to decide
what you should wear.
why do they get to say
"you aren't beautiful"
Why are they deciding for you
If you look too skinny
Too fat
Too dull or too bright
When they haven't lived in your body
Even for a minute.

Grief lives in the same places
Love, lived once.
You Losing something
Is nothing
But the evidence
Of you having it once.

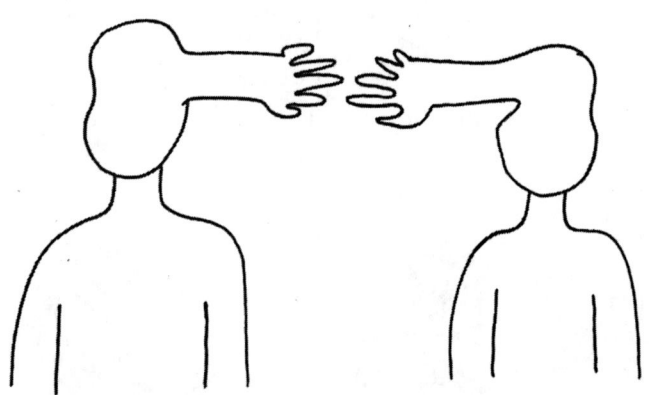

At the end of the day
All we want
Is someone
Who'd treat our pain
Like their own,

3:40 A.M. From heart to head

When the new lovers
Walk inside my heart
They see your name
Written all over the walls
Again, and again
Scratched to nothingness,
My efforts to forget you
Were so evident.

For the two powerful souls
Who raised me.
I have a bit of both of you
In me.
I wonder if I remind
You of yourself
Of your good parts
Of the bad parts
Of the human you could've become.
If I remind you
Of your childhood
If I remind you of your pain,
Your success,
Your unheard voices.
Am I the child you wanted to have
Or wanted to become
Do you live another life
Through me
Do you think
This is who you could have been,
Are you proud of me?

I was never afraid of losing people
I was always afraid of losing
The love they brought with them,
The warmth they brought with them,
The feeling of home in them,
I was afraid of
Never finding all of that
In some other human ever again.

To walk out
Of my home, which was you
Knowing that
I don't have any other place
To go
was the bravest thing
I have ever done.

3:40 A.M. From heart to head

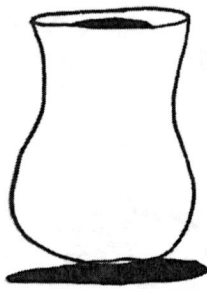

When I had you
There was no peace in that
And neither there was any peace
In losing you.

Your heartbreaks
And your heart aches
Not always come from
What other people
Did to you
Sometimes it comes from
The blame
You put on yourself
For letting all that happen.

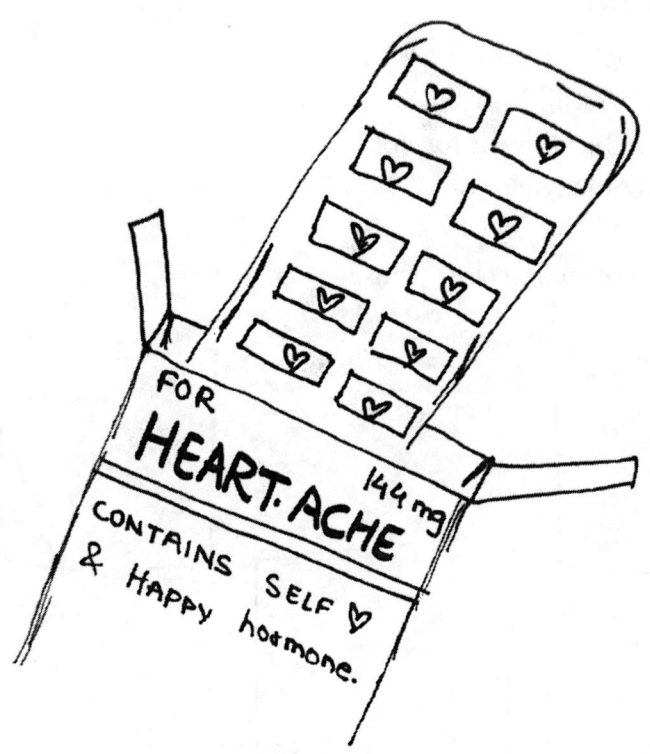

3:40 A.M. From heart to head

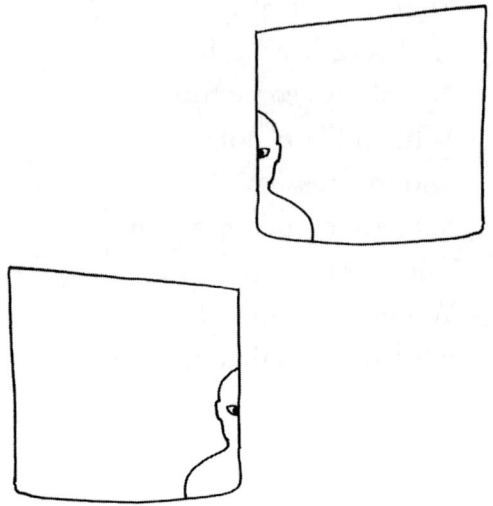

You left
 in such a confusing manner
That I still don't know
Whether to wait for you
To come back
Or walk
Into someone else's arms.

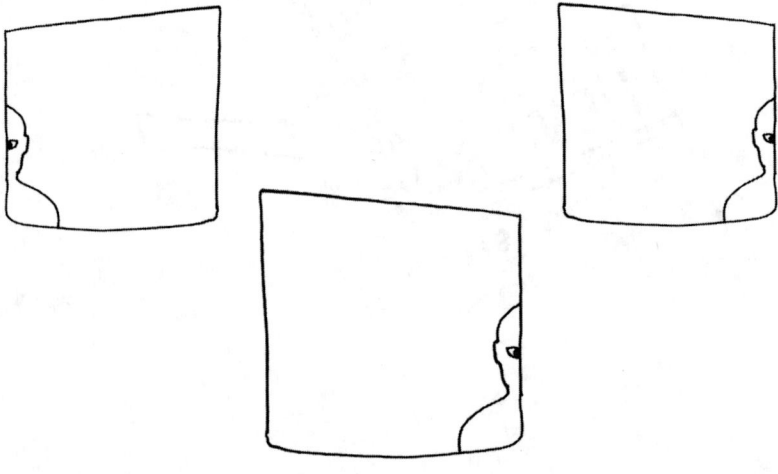

When I am wide awake
you never leave my mind
& When I am asleep
You are all that
I dream about.

You stuck around by me
When I was at my worst ,
And now that finally
It's time for my good times ,
You have left
Without getting the appreciation from me .
That you deserved all this time,
All these years
Can you come back for a second
So that I can say the thankyou
That I mean the most in my life.
So that I can say
That all these new people
Who walked in after you
Feel nothing like you.

[To my former best friend]

Life was either black or white
And I wanted to exist
In so many different colours.
It was either everything
Or nothing at all
And I wanted some days
Where I had
A little something
Of everything.

3:40 A.M. From heart to head

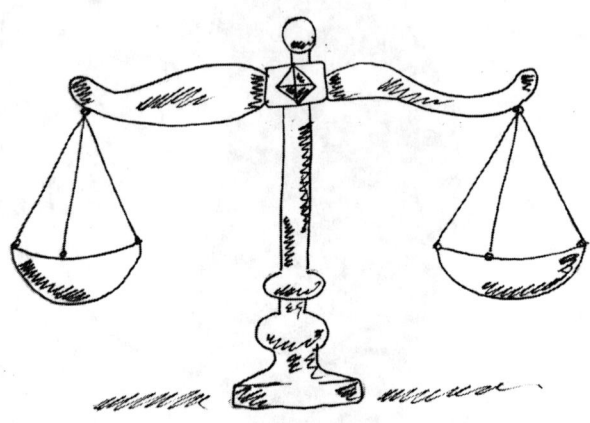

When you had to make a choice
Between me and the other things in life
You chose everything but me
And I
Chose you
Everyday
Even on days
When it was either to be with you
Or to be with me
I chose you over myself.

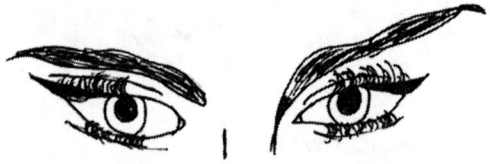

It's always in the eyes,
You can look into them
And know
If they are lying about loving you.
You can look into them
And know
That they have left
Way before they finally said it.

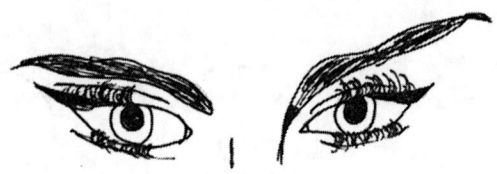

VOICES OF MY HEAD

depression was
a season of grief
The sadness that I did not want to talk about
Or share with anyone
Because I never thought anyone
Will even get it,
The way I get it.
If anyone will even understand
The language
In which the voices of my head
shatter me.

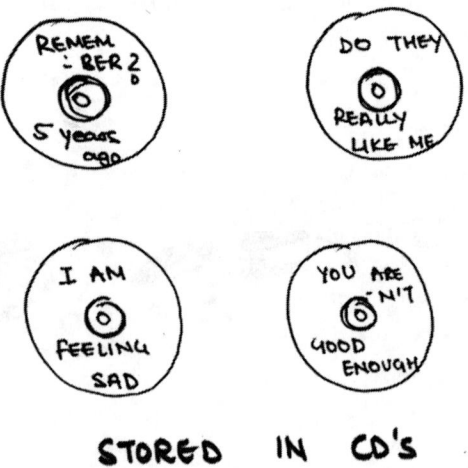

STORED IN CD'S

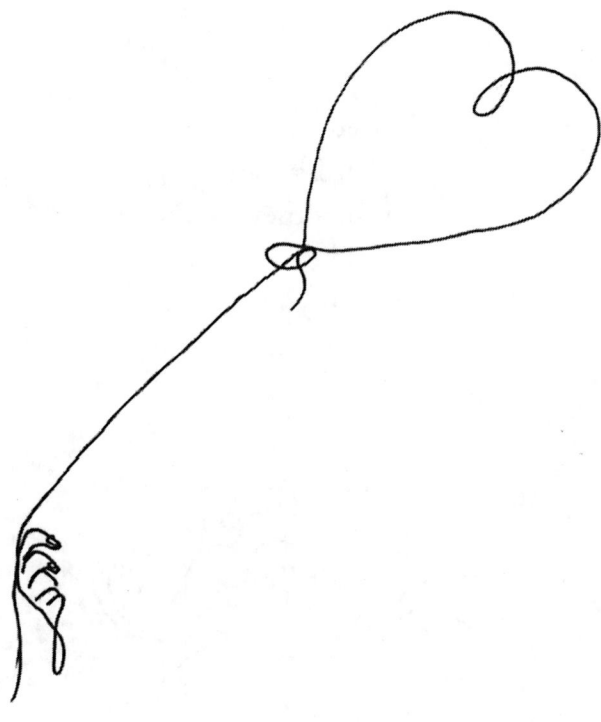

I left you behind
Still hoping
That may all the roads
That I am taking to walk away from you
Are the ones
That lead me to you.

I loved you so fiercely
That I became you
When they see me
They see you
And what you abandoned.
I loved you so fiercely
That I lost myself.

all the roads
that I took
to find myself,
I met heartbreak on every one of them
How can you find yourself
Without meeting grief
That you avoid.

(How can I meet mornings without living through darkest nights.)

3:40 A.M. From heart to head

I took my walls down for you
That took years to build
I changed the way I wear my shirt
The way I talked to people
The way I made friends
Only so that you could stay here comfortably
Even after all that I am now
After all I tried to be
You still didn't have it in you
To stay.
You owed me much more than that.

The paralysis that comes
With not having you around.
When every small task
Looks as difficult as moving a mountain.
When I have to remind myself to breathe
To smile
To eat
to get out of bed and walk around.
who were you?
who made me feel that
I could do everything
When I had you by my side.
And, nothing?
when I don't have you anymore.

(Heavy days, heavier nights)

Chapter: Head
(acceptance)

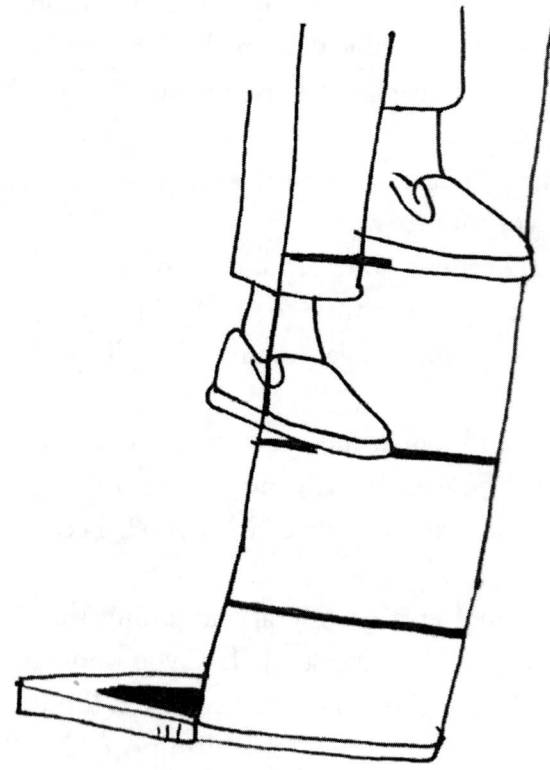

Things I want to tell my 14-year-old self

1. You'll be loved by so many people in unimaginable ways, but also
Walked upon, hurt, misunderstood, wronged and its okay because love will compensate for everything.
2. You'll meet people who will break your heart, and then you'll also meet people who will put all your broken pieces together.

3. There will be days when you'll feel lost and very far from yourself and there will be days when you'll come back to yourself. You'll always come back home.
4. Life will test your heart and trust me you'll emerge like a warrior.
5. You'll become the most beautiful woman you'll ever know, after your mother.
6. You'll think, keeping your emotions to yourself is healthy and the right thing to do but sometimes speaking about your baggage makes it a little less heavy.
7. They'll leave and sometimes you will, for the sake of your own peace. It will hurt, painfully, gut wrenchingly, but you will love, who you'll become after that.
8. Things won't matter after 5 years, anything that is stressing you out will evaporate before you know it.
9. You're the only one you've got. You can love, forgive, despise other people, but you'll realize no one will ever love you, like you can love yourself.
10. With every passing day, you'll fall in love with this journey more, than before and it will be hard, on some days to outwardly admit that you're feeling great but your life is beautiful and you'll know it.
11. & Most importantly you'll live to see all your dreams come to life.
12. You'll experience the lowest of the lows and the highest of the highs and it will take some time but you'll learn to embrace the duality of this life.

13. Your parents will become your best friends, on some days it will be hard to believe that if they even believe in you, but they do, they will be your biggest cheerleaders in all the races of life
14. You'll be alone, brutally alone on some nights and days, and at first you will hate it, but you'll realize you enjoy being with yourself and the thoughts of your head and the feelings in your heart.

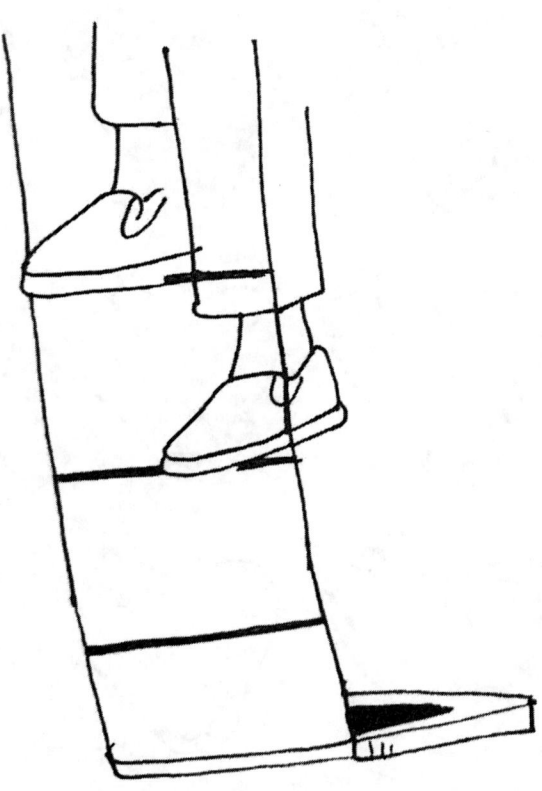

To be in love
Is to only be affected
By how much love
You have to offer
To The other person
And never how much
Love you're getting
In return.

[it's not a deal]

I don't want someone
To fight for me
To handle my issues
For me
To convince me that my bad days will end
I want someone to wait for me
While I do this all
For myself.

[*I need your love not your protection*]

I can't count
How many times
Someone has come and made me theirs
And have left me thinking
If I will ever belong to anyone else.
But I know
that I will always belong to me
If not anyone else ever again.
I know even if I come back to myself
A little late
The woman in me would still welcome me
With her arms open.

The real test of the love you have for yourself, happens on the day, when you're asked
To walk away from the only thing, that you love to death, because it takes away a little bit of you from you.

I hope
That once in your life
You experience a conversation
Like this
Where you say
That you have nothing left
To offer but your own self
And the person replies
With a big smile
" & That will be enough
That's all I need"

The real love
Was when you saw
How I cry over my work desk every day,
When you saw how I act
When I feel things aren't going according to me
When you saw me at my worst
Trying to make sense out of life.
When I had no will to exist
Where I won't shower or eat
When you saw my crying face
When you heard my anxiety talk
When you saw my fears come to surface
The real love for me
Was when you saw
Who I really am
And still made the decision to
Hold my hand forever.

3:40 A.M. From heart to head

I have made my peace
With every war that took place inside me.
I have made my peace
With every ending that I never saw coming
I have made my peace with
Your leaving and your never coming back
And now I am fine with every goodbye
& Me losing you
If that means me finding myself finally.

Love out of all the things
Is the most effortless
Emotion in this world.
If you have to ask for it,
Beg for it,
Lose your sleep for it,
Ruin your mind for it ,
You are waiting for it
In the wrong place.

3:40 A.M. From heart to head

I hope
That you are not
Willing
To settle for someone
Who calls you
Sunshine
When you are
Literally
The sun itself.

You are a big, vast sky,
Endless and infinite,
So beautiful
& Everything that has ever broken you
Or will ever break you
Is a tiny cloud,
& One day the winds will carry these clouds
Far away.
But you'll always stay here.
You're the only permanent thing
About this temporary life.

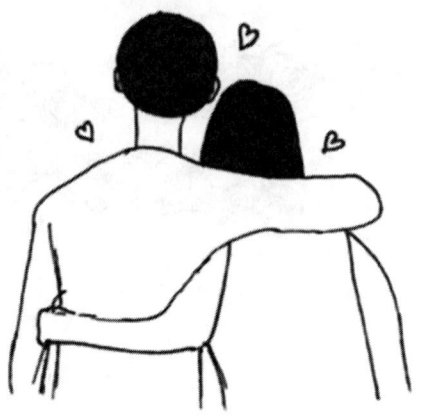

His greatness
Did not make me
Feel small.
It made me believe
In my ability
To be great,
Just like him.

– The right kind of love

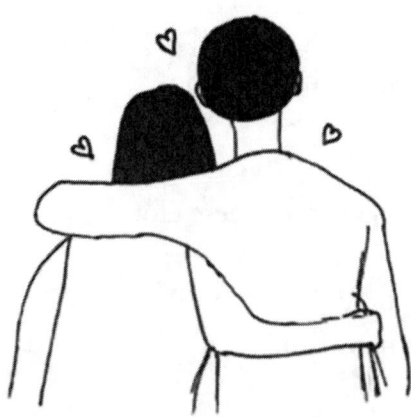

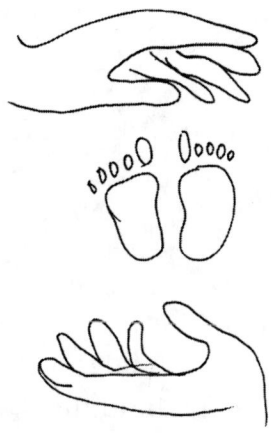

I hope
You get to come back here,
In another life,
Just to live a little more.
Because I know
That you spent your current life,
Sacrificing for me.
I wish
You live a life, long enough to see,
How happy my life got
Just because ,
At some point
You decided
To not give up.

(To my parents< my makers)

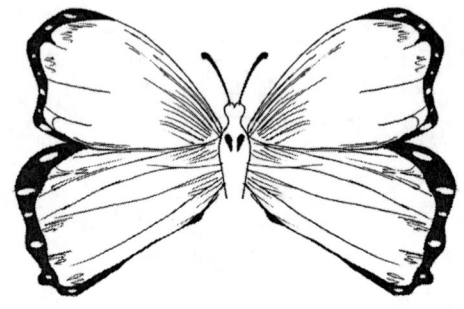

Endings,
Are beautiful.
With everything making sense,
With you understanding
The beginning a little better.
The best place to be
Is to be at the finishing line
Of a wonderful life
Or a wonderful book.

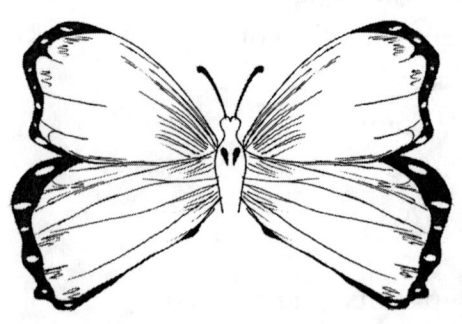

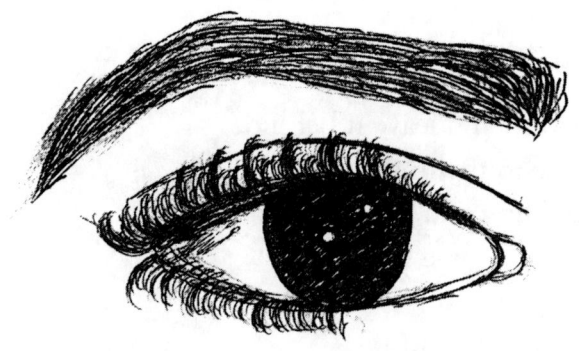

I recognize
Two days of my life
As the best ones
the day
I met you
And the day
I met me.

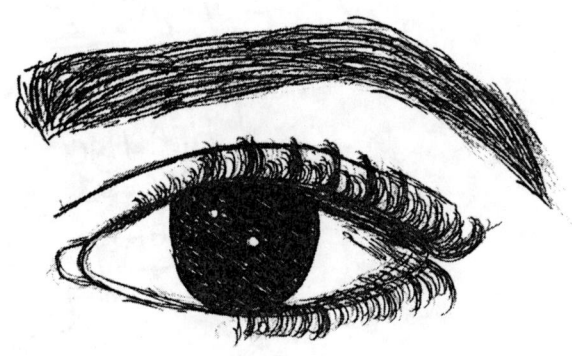

3:40 A.M. From heart to head

I can make it easy for you
by telling you,
that grief never leaves,
It's us who choose
to move forward and leave it behind.
so, if you have something,
which is troubling you,
which messes with you daily.
Then there are chances
that you are holding onto it
more than
It is holding onto you.

[the two-way relationship
between us and the things
that made us who we are]

This poem
Is a hug
Made out of words
So, if you read this
This is just me hugging you
Because I know it has been hard
I know you are trying your best.
And I know that I can't take your bad days away
But I hope this makes you feel
a little less sad than yesterday.

Hearing my name
From you
Gave my existence
A new different meaning.
It was
As if I was born again
No one takes it
The way you do.
No one does it like you.

[love]

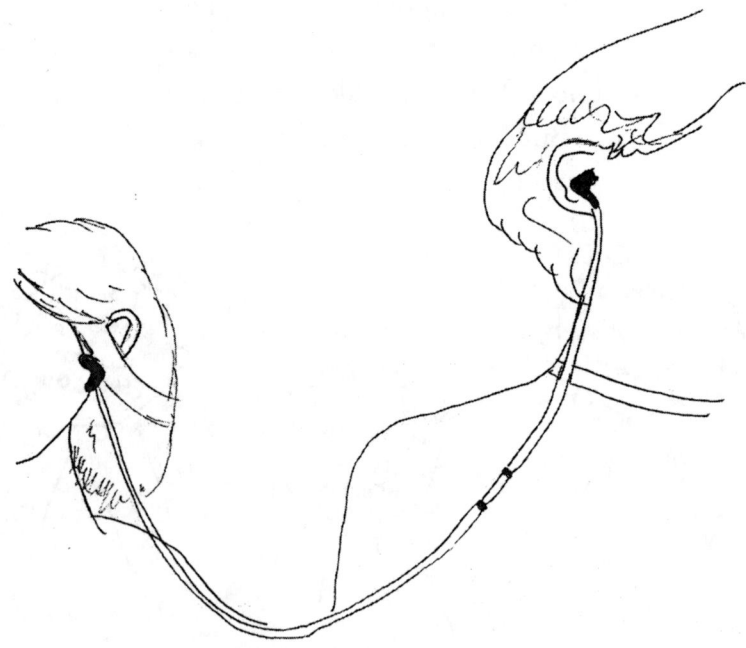

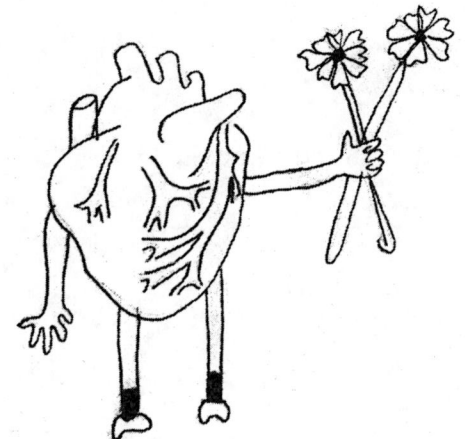 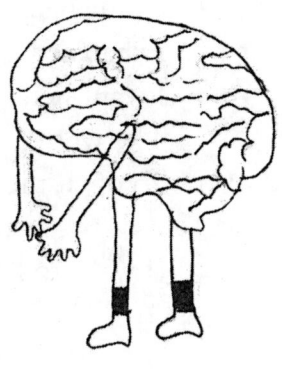

If ever your mind asks you
On your darkest of nights
If love actually exists?
If you will ever find it?
then keep your hand
On your chest
And let your mind feel and hear
Every beat of your heart
And tell it
That love exists
And it is beating inside your chest.
And even if you don't find love in someone else
At least you found it in yourself.

3:40 A.M. From heart to head

After being lost for years
When I finally
Come back home,
Exhausted.
I want her,
The woman who I always wanted to be,
To open the door for me.

(I want to know if it was worth it)

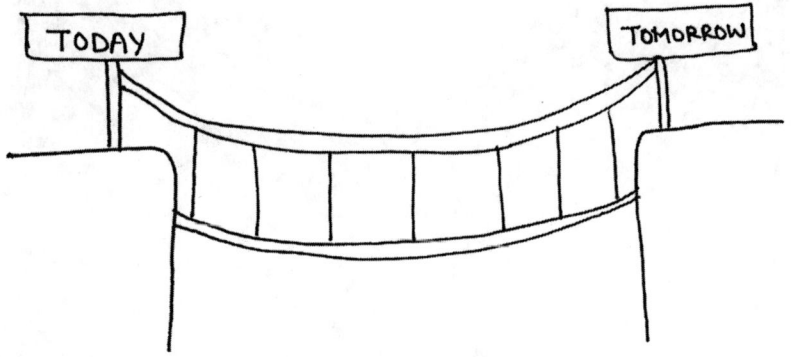

I know
That we all are same
I know that we feel
That we are nights with no mornings
But I also know
That we will make it out of this chaos
Even if we spend the rest of our lives
Wondering
How we did it.
But we all will.
At the end.

Trauma

And one morning
Hope
Came to meet me
And never left.

[*it lives in me*]

"When you speak to me, my body, my mind, my soul & my heart,
everyone listens. Everything inside me goes silent.
Your voice echoes inside me for days. You bring a pin drop silence with you
In my very loud existence."

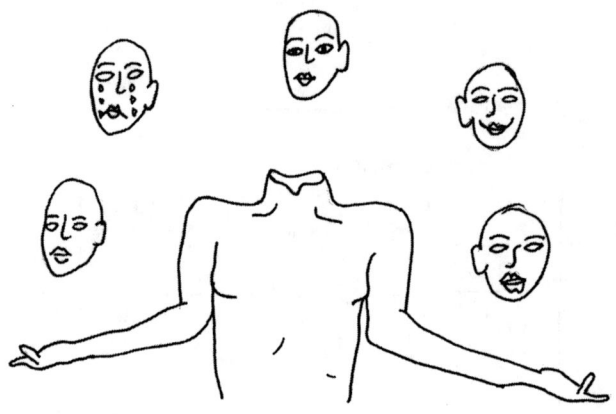

The most
Beautiful place
To be
Is to be in love
With our own self.

I want you to
See far in your future
Far enough
To see the days
Where everything is alright
Where you are happy
Where there is no trace
Of what once happened
Of who you once were.

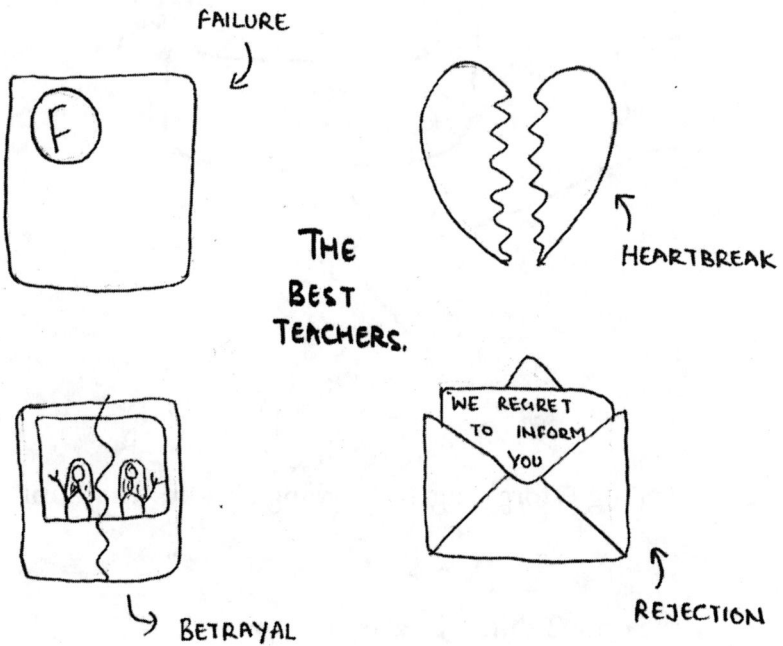

Healing = forgiving + not going back to what broke you

[the only 2 things it takes to move on]

Everyone tells me
How great of an honor
It must be to be a writer.
To be able to give words
To what your mind says.
But wish I could tell everyone
That how extraordinary
It must be
To be the muse.
People who get written about
Every now and then, some poems
On their eyes
And some about the way they talk .
Imagine
Just existing
And someone translates the way you breathe
In pretty words.

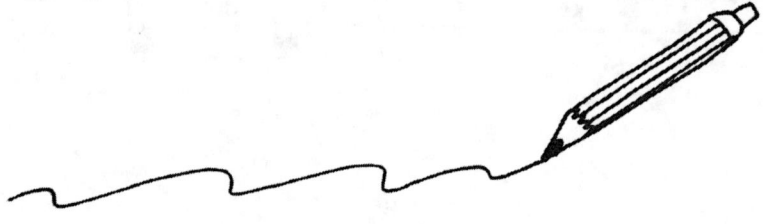

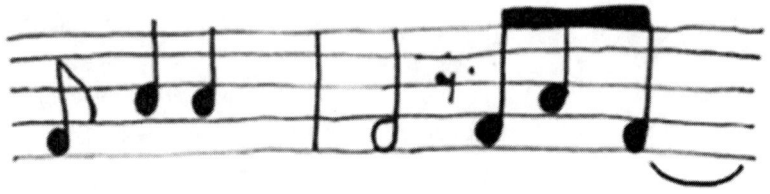

You are the poem
I know by heart.
You are the song
I have learnt well enough
To never forget.

I don't want to be
Someone else
I don't want to have
Someone else's eyes
Or smile or hair or voice
Or skin or color or gender
To feel amazing
When I can just
Look at my own reflection
And take my own breath away.

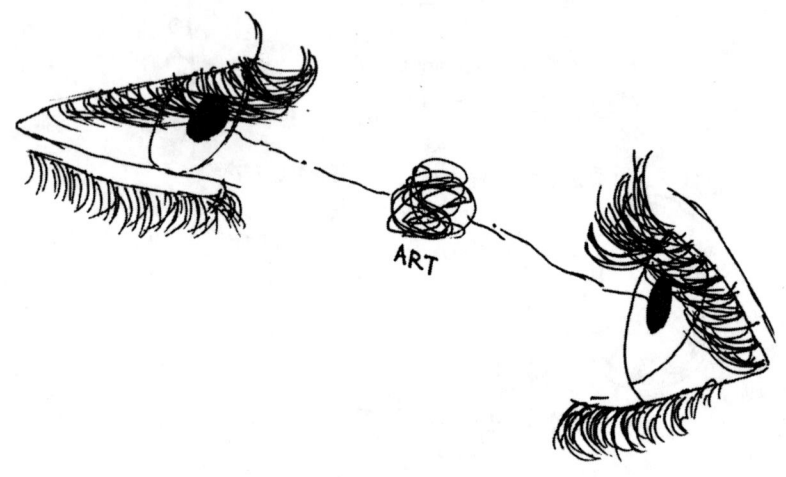

The best part
About looking
In your eyes
Is that
I never feel
I should be looking
Somewhere else.

–The art of eye contact

Growing up, me and my sister always loved different kind of things, our sources of happiness came from two different worlds. For me it would be buying pink and black dresses, for her it was her favourite food and movies. But she helped me learn a lot about candies and the best places to eat at town, and I taught her what earrings would go the best with her dresses. Our differences made us love each other more, because they were so well accommodated, I wonder if I can do this with her, then why can I not do this with the person, I have to spend my entire life with, how can I part ways with someone just because we aren't similar enough. If I fall in love with someone, only to realize that he loves different things about a movie, is there a greater honor, that we appreciate different things about this life, yet we come back to each other at the end of the day.

(Our differences teach us that we can so deeply love some people and some things, even when they look nothing like us.)

How can we say
We are alone
When we have
Our heart beating for us every day
Our mind speaking to us every moment
Our lungs breathing for us
Every second
This is not being alone
Alone is when
Even the insides of you go silent
When you feel
as if you live with you
But you haven't heard from yourself
Since years.

I'd rather regret
Not letting someone in ,
Returning to an empty home.
Rather than regretting letting my walls
Down for someone
Who was never worth all the magic I gave him.

To: the small grief

We spend our lives, disregarding the small things, because we think it is too tiny to be even cared about. We convince ourselves that we don't deserve to be upset because the reason behind it is trivial, because others have it worse than us. We invalidate our sadness, go and sit in denial.
Even if you are grieving about something which might look insignificant to others, even if you hear this from everyone that life will give you 100 chances. You can take all of your time with it, and deal with it the way you want to. Because when it comes to giving, life will not give 100 but a thousand reasons to be happy again, but take your time to celebrate loss, you really don't have to rush out of anything.
It's okay and its normal.
You and all that you feel, is valid.

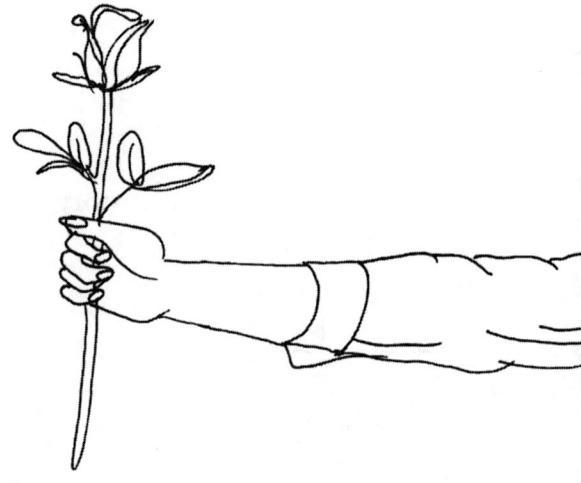

When I am broken,
You are
What keeps me together.
When life seems hard
You are
Who makes it look a little easy.
In the world
Where I am willing to let go of everything.
You are
What looks worth holding on to.
You are everything better
About this life, that I am living.
Because in this lifetime
Every time my mind makes me believe
That I am unknown
You make me feel
identified.

–You make me feel like I am the only one with a name
In the land of all unnamed things.

And never in the history of heartbreaks
The broken
has remained broken
For life.

—We are destined to be whole

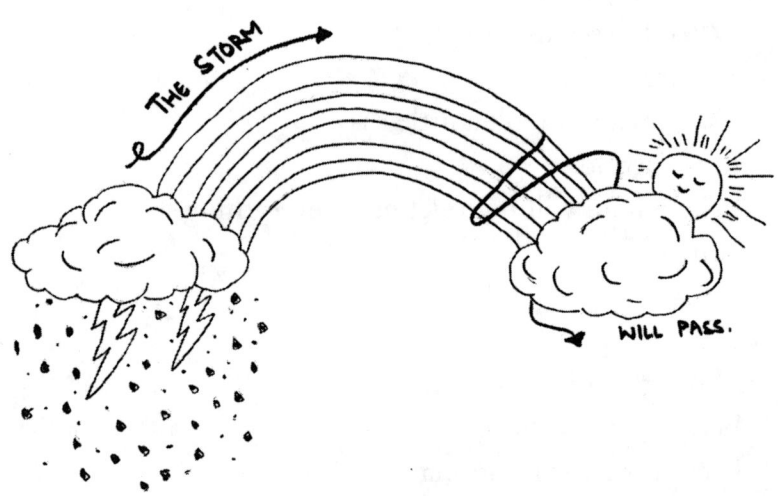

This skin is just protecting
What's inside me
So, what if it is scarred
If it is stretched enough to have marks
If it is thick or thin
If it is darker or lighter
If I am not proud of who I am
From within
Then why am I concerned
About how I look from outside.

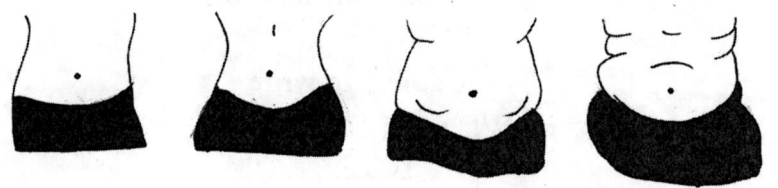

3:40 A.M. From heart to head

When I count my blessings
I count
The ability to write
Whenever I want to,
Twice.
Because how amazing it is
That whenever
I sit down with pen & paper
I always have
Something to express
How amazing it is
To know
That universe uses me
Every day for this art.
I am an artist every day.

You say you hate them now
You don't
You just don't know
What to do
With the love you have for them
Now that
They aren't here to witness it anymore.

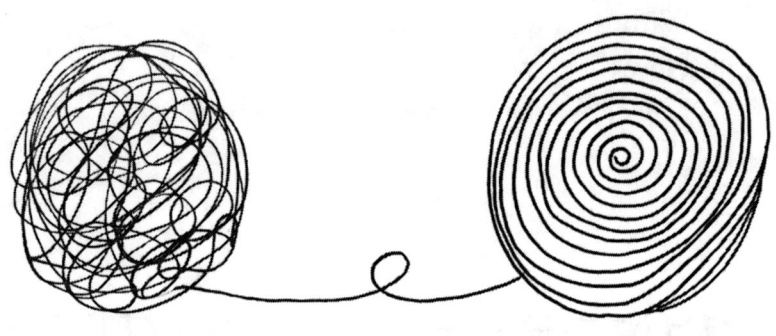

I saw people
Swearing on their deathbeds
That life gets better.
So, I know for sure this one thing
That my good days will be here
Before all of my days end,
And that's a hope to have.

"like every burn on your skin, like every cut on your hand, like every broken bone, your heart too, will heal one day. For, it is also a part of your body For, we are humans, & our injuries heal. It may leave behind a scar but it no longer pains."

[the story behind your wounds]

I am a human but there are so many days
I don't allow myself to be one.
I force a smile on my face
And I force enthusiasm on my mind
I tell myself to be my ideal self
When for me
Ideal self is feeling nothing
But happiness.
And just shove my other emotions
To a quiet corner of my body,
Leaving them unattended for days, months and years .
Telling them on their face,
That "shut up, you are insignificant" Or maybe worse,
like "you are not needed" but just like the woman I am,
 They have my fire in them.
That's why time & time again
They come on surface to threaten me.
That they will roar out one day
Exposing my lies of being happy every day.
That they will injure the image people have of me
That they will tell the world who I really am.
And then I beg to them
To not reveal to the world
That I am a human.

And that its impossible for me
To admit that yes I am not fine and that life has not been great lately
When nothing goes in my favour.
And that's when these emotions and voices of my alter ego
Feel pity for me
That's when they tell me
That being human is my biggest strength,
My biggest gift ,
And I am born to flaunt it,
I am born to bare open my soul in front of everyone
And tell them
I feel it all
And that's because
 I have a beating heart
And breathing lungs.
I am created to do a million things
So why do you think
I am made
To feel only one emotion?
Out of the 100 million other emotions that I can feel.

[your humanity is not your weakness]

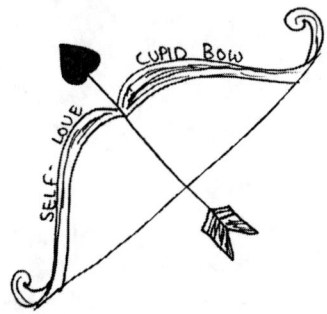

Growing up
I hated that I am a woman
Because I always thought
We had to endure so much,
To the extent it felt unfair,
To the extent I felt that the other gender has it easy.
But it's so different to be a woman than calling yourself one,
And when I finally became one.
I realised, me ability to endure everything, was an indicator of how powerful I was
Of how much strength I had in me
Now I can't think of one thing about myself
Which makes me prouder.

{It's natural to dislike an unfinished painting, you haven't fully become the woman you're supposed to be, embrace your womanhood)

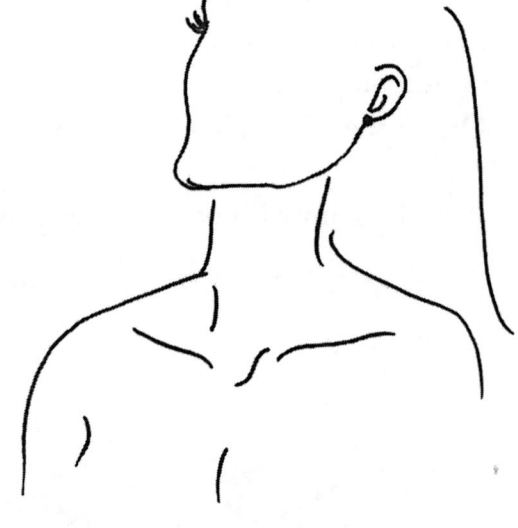

When important things
Come to an end.
Like a 3 year old relationship,
Or a lifelong friendship,
Or your favourite tv series,
Or a job ,
Or someone close's life.
You sit with yourself,
Teaching yourself,
How to be without them
From that point onwards,
By embracing other things in your life.
It's important,
& It's okay if you take longer than usual,
To learn,
To grieve,
To feel ready again,
To sit for a few moments,
To cherish the happy time,
You had with it.
You are on a very special journey
Take your time
& Do it right.

If the ocean
Who is a thousand billion years old,
Can be wild
& be desired for it,
Then in my defence
I am just 21.

[never apologise for your wildness]

He was the strongest for me,
When he cried.
I wish he knew
That everything
he held back, because he thought
It makes him look weak
Are the only things
That made him the bravest for me.
[to men: your tears don't take away your masculinity]

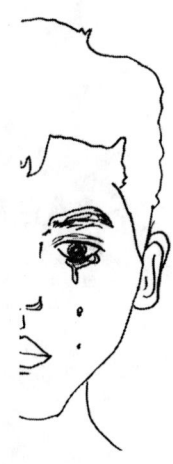

Before you decide to love again
Make sure to heal & rest.
From your past
Else, you will end up
Expecting them to heal
Your wounds
Which were yours to heal all this time.

(no one can carry your baggage better than you)

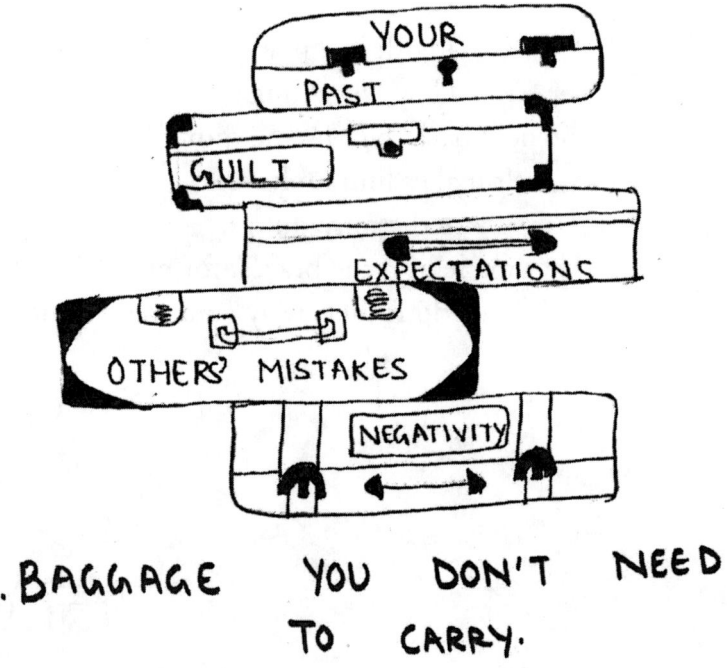

Urja Joshi

All this time, when people did not understand me, I thought maybe there is something wrong with me. Maybe I am hard to be with, hard to love or maybe I am the problem. But if I knew then, what I know now. I'd understand that it was not me, it was them who needed repairing all this time. because a damaged heart sees damage everywhere.
And I am grown now,
 I am wise now,
I know now that no one can put me down, if I don't let them.

[your healing is your responsibility]

Growing up
Is nothing else
But knowing
When to close some doors,
& To say that
"I really did try my best."
At the right time.

[closure]

I met me today
& It felt like,
Healing meeting hurting .
I know she dealt with chaos,
I know it has been hard for her,
But I am sure
She was happy to see what I've become.
I know that even if for a second,
It made sense to her,
That why this all happened
The way it did.

[you're your own hope]

(& Nowhere is lonely
If you belong to yourself enough.)

can you imagine a room
where,
Every great thing
That has ever happened to you,
exists.
& Is the person who hurt you the most
Standing in there?

(It left the biggest void in you, because it mattered so much/ you owe them your greatest gratitude.)

3:40 A.M. From heart to head

When you've no love for yourself,
The other person can see
That in your eyes,
In the way you talk about your body
In the way you hide your face, when someone wants to talk about
How beautiful you are.
They learn how to love you from the way you love yourself
They start talking to you,
The way they've heard you talk about yourself.
Your journey of finding the right one
Starts with realizing that
They can't love you,
The way you can love yourself.
They can't fill the void, that you've
Created by not loving yourself.

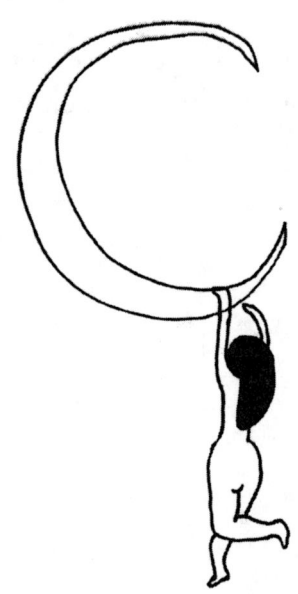

I don't know you
But I do know
That you don't deserve to wait for someone
Who left you behind.
You need someone who'd take you with them
On every adventure
Life has to offer.

3:40 A.M. From heart to head

You will survive
Every loss
That you've ever been through
But that one time
When you lose yourself
Briefly.
It's so hard to breathe
Those days.
When the rock bottom becomes your new home
When days go by so fast
Because you aren't living in the moments
We aren't designed to survive those kind of days
And if you've ever touched that
And you've come back
You've no idea
Who you are.
You've no idea of your power.

[depression survivors]

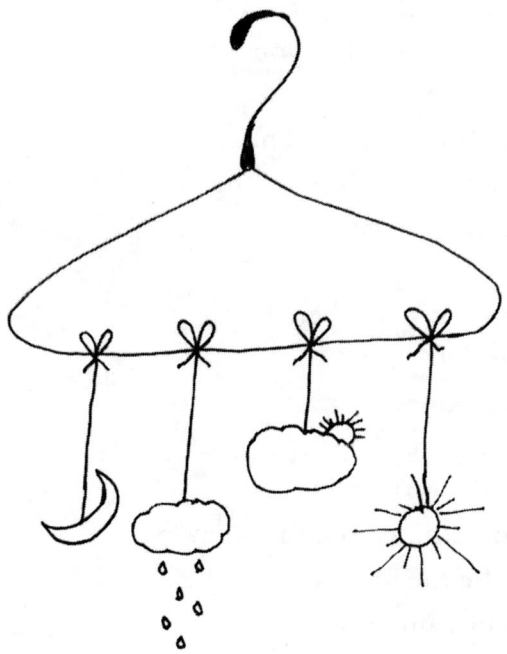

The human tragedy

I have a list of things
And people who make me so happy,
That I forget I was ever grieving.
But like the human I am
My happiness also wants to know
If I affect them just the same.
If I make them happy too
If the sun waits to see me
Just like I do,
 every morning,
To see him.

We are so connected that
Sometimes the grief in you
Is generational,
Inherited from your parents,
Which they were given by theirs,
And you can't trace it
That at what time
Someone was so bothered
That they left
But their sadness
Is still living inside you.
And if you don't decide
To do something about it today
You will be the reason
The coming ones too
Will grieve like this
For reasons
They did not know
And for decisions
They did not take.

(Trauma is passed down, generation to generation//
break the cycle)

Everything I've left behind in life,
For good,
For bad,
I still revisit them,
To miss them a little loud on some days.
To tell them
That I still love you,
But I love me more now.

[I am learning]

I wish I knew you
When you were 13.
I'd know exactly what to say,
So that you don't grow up
Hating your body.
I'd know exactly what to do,
So that you feel safe around older men.
I'd know exactly how to wipe your tears,
So that you don't believe
To show emotion is to be weak.
Our lives would be so easy
If we learnt the right lessons
When we were young.
If someone held us,
Just the way we needed to be.
If we found home early in life.
So that we don't have to spend our adulthood
Looking for home in other people.

[you become who you needed back then]

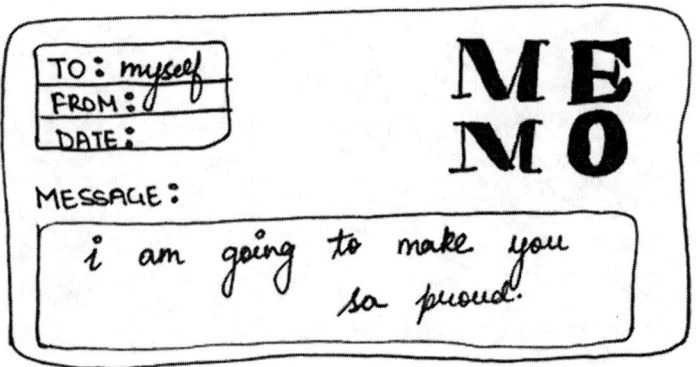

If every ending
Is the beginning
Of something
Else.
Then your leaving
Is the
Arrival of
Someone even better.

PAST

- - - - - - - - - - - - - - - - -

YOU

Would your past self
Trust
This version of yours
With their
Life and its decisions.
You promised that version that
You'll be happier,
That you'll Choose better people for you,
That you'll take care of yourself.
Are you keeping your promises?
Are you smiling back at them?
Knowing you became
Who you needed
Back then.

Urja Joshi

You will never be too young
To love someone deeply,
To feel grief,
To feel hopeless about life,
To be expert at what you do,
To understand loss.
If your heart feels something,
If it beats faster because of how anxious you feel.
Then don't let anyone tell you that,
You're not supposed to feel what you're feeling,
Just because you haven't lived enough years
On this planet.
You don't have to wait
to be understood
Till you are old enough,
For this world.

[you deserve love]

3:40 A.M. From heart to head

When head and heart
Fell in love with each other
They realized
They will always view life
So differently.
One will always think
And the other will always feel
Always trying to make each other
Like themselves.
But to love is to realize
That they have
What you don't.
If you feel a lot on some days
Then their thinking will balance it for you.
You don't have to spend the rest of your life changing them
Because to love
Is to love them
Exactly the way they are.

When I missed you,
I did it with my whole existence.
With the over loving in my heart,
 and overthinking of my head.
But when I left you behind,
I made sure to wipe you
Out of my memory.
Now they talk of you
And I can't remember the days
When you used to be my everything.

3:40 A.M. From heart to head

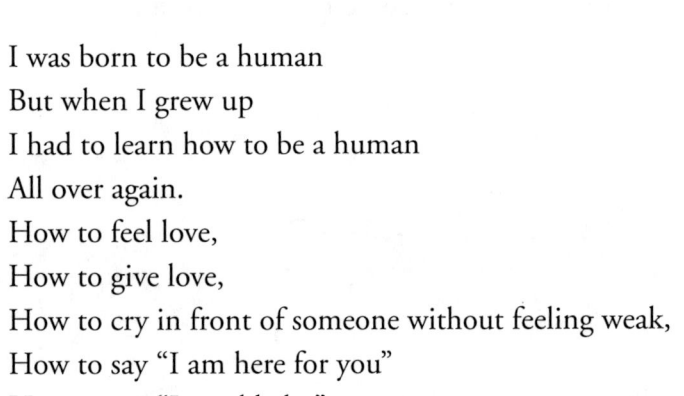

For who I am becoming

I was born to be a human
But when I grew up
I had to learn how to be a human
All over again.
How to feel love,
How to give love,
How to cry in front of someone without feeling weak,
How to say "I am here for you"
How to say "I need help."
How to take compliments without feeling they might be lying.
When I grew up, I had to ask myself
If I have ever known anything at all.

They don't believe you when you're a male,
And they say you'll forget it,
When you're young.
They say it's your fault,
When you're a woman.
And they say,
"You asked for it"
When you wear skirts.
They say you will never find love,
When you say it out loud.
And they say "it happened years ago get over it"
When you tell them you still can't sleep
Thinking about it.
And sometimes,
They say it never happened,
When you have only words to prove yourself.
You did not deserve it,
The touch without your consent,
And the gaze on your body
Without you wanting it.
But you are living today
Despite of it,
Trying to forget that it happened.
It was a part of the past,
It is not a part of you.
You're more than what happened to you
And we're so proud of you.

Even the most beautiful faces
Were left for someone else
And abandoned
By what they thought will last forever.
As humans we all will at some point
Will not be chosen by someone
The way we choose them.
But the doors of your heart
Should always be open for yourself
When you want to come back.
After being disappointed by life.

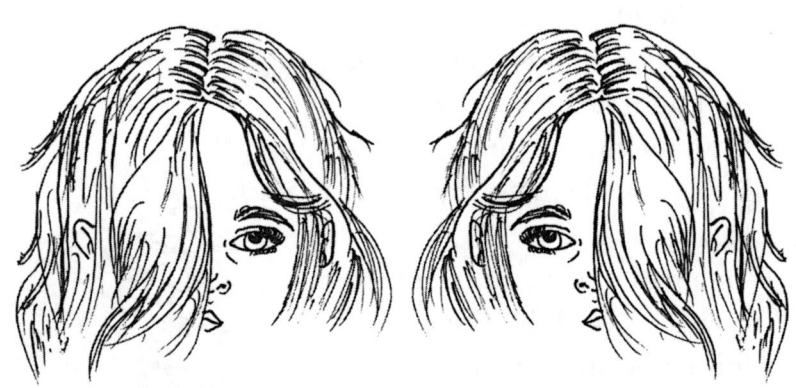

I hope to not
Forget my grief.
I want to sit with it,
Understand it,
And become friends with it.
So that I can
Carry what broke me,
With me for the rest of my life
In the most beautiful manner.

I bet on broken hearts,
On the day
When I finally meet happiness,
And content,
I will still look at the door
Hoping
If you're about to arrive too.

It's time to bid farewell
To every person
Who looked like a forever
But was not.
To the person
You once were
But not anymore.
It's time to say a goodbye.
To every thing
That you are waiting for to come back
But deep down you know
It won't.

*The only reason
I want to be with someone
Is to add love
In my life
That I already have for myself.
And to not make me feel less alone,
I don't want to
Start my happily ever after
Just because
I am tired of being with myself.*

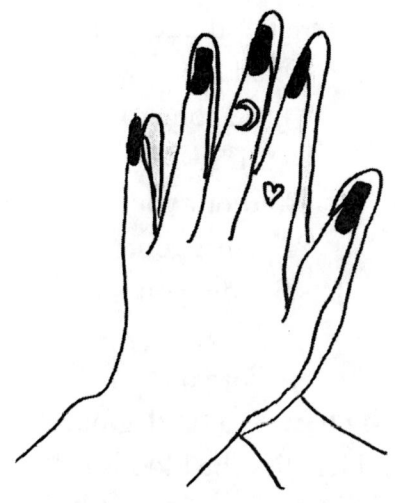

I hope you fall in love
Not because it was lonely on weekends,
Or it was convenient,
Or they were the only one around,
Or you wanted a family,
Or both of you talked about your broken heart to each other.
I hope love falls for you,
Because you had so much meaning in your life that,
You couldn't wait to give it to someone
Without ever thinking of getting anything in return.

3:40 A.M. From heart to head

My heart is a battleground
Here lies the remains
Of all the wars
I have gone to,
With you,
Without you,
Against you,
Besides you,
&
For you.
My heart is a battleground,
Here lies the bloodshed
Of all the versions of me,
The army of people I once was
The army of humans
I'll ever be.

Urja Joshi

Even when
We met for the first time,
He looked familiar
More than any person
I've ever known.
And I asked
"Have we met before?"
And he answered
"Maybe, in other life"
& I think this is what happens
When two soulmates meet
It's just like
Coming back to home
After a long day out.

And why are we conditioned
To feel this way
That
We will never get there
if we are not anywhere by today.
& Just because your time
Has not come yet
Does not mean it will never come.

[nothing happens in a day]

I watched him
Walk towards me.
And I smiled
Because I knew
That I might have forgotten what happened last time
Because that might be the only reason,
I feel love for someone
Once again today.

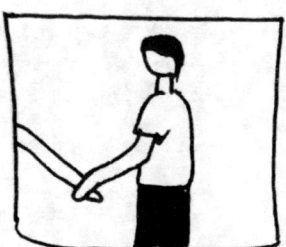

Chapter : Soul
(letters from the diary)

For
the person I once was.
(*Why am I, the way I am*)

3:40 A.M. From heart to head

When you're growing up, it's hard to look back and be proud of who you once were. Acceptance, love, forgiveness, kindness are some of the many emotions, which flow so effortlessly to us when we have to offer these to other people, but it becomes equally harder to pull these emotions out of us when it comes to our own selves.

To accept who I once was, to love that person, to forgive that human, I learnt all of this with so much difficulty.

Dear you, I know our past is filled with mistakes we regret, and things we want to change, I know you're the version of me, which I have left behind, you're also the version of me, which I am so harsh on, you must feel so unloved by me, only because when I get reminded of you, I also get reminded of my weak parts. But I also know, that it was not your fault in any way, to be so naïve, to not know the true intentions of this world, it was not your fault that you let people walk all over you, you thought they'd do the same for you, it was not your fault for being so vulnerable, that you waited for people to pay you attention, so that you can tell them everything that doesn't feel right lately, it was not your fault for being so driven by your kind heart that you almost forgot that you have a head which can take decisions for you. you loved so fearlessly, not caring if it would betray you the next day, you expressed so bravely, not caring what this world will think of you, you felt so much, not caring about how overwhelmed you'd become eventually. You were everything I want to be now, you are sitting in the past now, and I know there are so many aspects I regret having back then, but leaving you behind also costed me so many goods.

I don't feel now, I only think, I don't forgive now, I only move on with life, I don't love now, I only play it safe, I don't talk now, I only respond back & I don't express now, I keep everything to me. Its so funny that I used to think, everything I was, was my biggest curse, to feel so much, to love so much, to give so much. But now I feel so limited, so held back by my own body and soul, now I feel I'd do anything to be you again, I'd do anything to feel something in my heart.

So many losses, one after another, and feeling so much grief, that I ended up closing the gates of my heart, this way that I don't know how to open them again. The new lovers don't give me butterflies anymore, the new friends don't win my trust anymore, the new experiences aren't exciting me anymore. To think that 4 years ago, this version of me, was all who I wanted to be, to be awfully unaffected and unbothered by everything, to experience the kind of happiness which remains unshaken by someone's presence or absence, but now that I am finally this human, it has never felt hollower.

I was sent on this earth to feel everything, and I spent years convincing myself that if i could just shut down my feelings for a while, it'd be so great, but isn't feeling it all, is what makes us human beings, isn't shutting down our heart, will mean us living a little less.

What is a bigger tragedy than to have a heart but to not put it into use for loving. if I could, I'd do and give anything to be myself again, even if it means me being weaker.

I am sorry if you felt unwanted by me, but you're the version of me that I am the proudest of, I am so proud that I was once you, that you are nothing but a part of me. I am so proud that I am one of those few people who can look back and smile at the life they've lived.

I know now that why I am the way I am, but it's not who I want to be. I want to be 16-year-old again, hurt but at least I know how to cry without feeling like I just ripped open my clothes in front of stranger, at least I was sure of who I wanted to be in life, at least I was stubborn enough to love the wrong one, at least I was hopeful of nothing going wrong in life. I love who I grew into but I love more the person I grew from, the person I was.

For
days when I struggle to like my company.

3:40 A.M. From heart to head

Dear you,

I have lived so many years with you, yet I don't think that I am used to being with you. Whenever I have an opportunity to sit down with no one else but me, I call it loneliness, I think it's bad that on some days, the only voice I can hear talking to me, is the voice of my head.

I feel bad for me when I find out that there have been days and there will be days when only I can understand myself. My whole life I have searched for me in other people, someone who thinks like me, who listens to the same kind of music I do, someone whose favourite color is what my favourite color is, someone who says yes to the things I like, and hates the same people I can't stand. I have always found myself so not enough, that I always needed someone else to do things with, as if being with me was a curse, as if my company is so bad, especially when I am so young, especially when my whole life is in front of me, waiting for me to live it. When days will get hard, when the job will get tiring, when my partner will want space, where will I go if I don't feel comfortable with myself enough to sit with myself and ask myself if there is anything about my day that I'd like to go through for the second time.

where will I go on days when everyone who I rely on will be tired of me relying on them, who will I speak to, on days when everyone who I love will find other people to love, who will I go to movies with when all my friends will be busy. There could be so many things I don't see coming at this moment, but if I can't rely on myself then who can I rely on? if I am uncomfortable with myself then how will I spend the rest of my life with someone else, if I don't love myself then how will I accept others who love me, it all starts with how we are with ourselves, how we behave, speak, listen to us, and it will always end on us.

it will not matter in 10 years how the world treated us, we will be left with ourselves, and if we don't like the person we become, then how will we spend those days when we will have no one but our shadows.

Dear you I am learning to love you, in a way, where being with you won't eat me from inside, where it won't be the reason why I can't sleep at night, where I wouldn't force people in my life because I think I am lonely. I am trying to get to a place where I'd be able to say that I love when I am with other people who love me, but I love it even more when I am all by myself because who can love me better than myself, the body that I live in, the soul in me that experiences this life.

I hope I am able to make myself understand that being alone isn't as bad as I think, it's a gift, there will be years in my life when I will wish for even 5 minutes with myself, and here when I actually have them, I am busy looking for reasons to spend them with someone else, on something else.

 Don't I have an entire life to be somewhere else, then why am I hating it if life is giving me time to be by myself completely, let me cherish it, before I lose it, before I am living again, before I am regretting it.

Often when we find ourselves all alone, with no one around, but us, in our own company, it's a reminder, to give the love, you gave to your lover, the loyalty you gave to your best friend, the respect you offered to your parents, the helping hand you extended towards that needy stranger, your kindness, every good thing about you, to yourself. It's always going to be uncomfortable sitting with yourself, if you aren't familiar enough with who that person is, there shouldn't be the awkward silence of two strangers, between you and yourself.

What is love
If not
Chosen insanity.

[Zara]

Acknowledgements

As I wrap up this life transforming project, a book, that has seen my laughs, my tears, my most vulnerable conversations, people who came & went. I want to take a moment to thank each and every one who has been a part of this wonderful journey.

It's a miracle in itself that I am finally releasing this book to the world after a long 3-year hiatus, after a long time, I am so happy to be a writer again and I couldn't have done this without the support of my parents. Mom & Dad, I have never loved anyone in my life more than you. Thank you so much for believing in me when even I lost faith.

Thankyou Aastha, my little sister, well not so little anymore, you've always been my loudest cheerleader and my best friend on my lonely days.

Thank you so much to my entire team at anecdote publishing house for making this book, a dream come true. From the cover designers to the editors, the publishing team to the paper producers, I owe you my everything.

Sagar sir, where do I even start, you saw my talent

way before I did, the storytelling in my poetry, and the beauty in my books more than I as a creator ever could, you are the only reason I had the courage to put out 3:40 am after 3 long years. Thank you so much!

I'm so thankful to the PAPERBAAG for believing in my vision and bringing it to life by creating this beautiful cover, no one could've done it better than you.

My entire friend crew, I love you guys, thanks for always bombarding me with "when are you releasing the book?". Thank you for being patient with me when I immersed myself into the process and forgot to be a friend to you.

MY READERS, I know this has been rough for you, you haven't heard from me for a while, but I promise to make this journey memorable. Thank you so much for being so understanding and so patient with me, when I took my time with this masterpiece. You're the most amazing community to exist and the best thing that has ever happened to me. Thank you for making me a writer. This is for you. There are no writers without readers. There is no Urja Joshi without you

Dear universe, thank you so much for letting me create and deliver, thank you for blessing me with the ability to write and express, my life would've been so different and difficult if I didn't have this to go to, at the end of my days.

While I am at it, I'd like to give the credits to the

musical art video directed by my favourite Kendrick lamar for "count me out" which inspired the opening verse of zara in 3:40 a.m.

And at the very end, thank you "3:40 a.m." for choosing me to be your creator, for adding more beauty to my author's catalogue. I am so proud of you and I am still in disbelief that you're now born after all these years.

Thank you to the woman I was when I first came up with the idea of this book and thankyou to the woman I've become, now that I am finally releasing it.

I hope you had a life changing read, just like I had a life changing release.

Thank you! thank you! thank you!

Urja Joshi
(Truly yours because
I don't think I've ever belonged
This well
To anyone before."

About the Author

Born in year 2001, on 28th July. Urja joshi is a young published author, illustrator, podcaster, song writer, performer, speaker, and much more. Her interest in writing runs back to an early age of 7. She created an Instagram account and started her professional writing by posting small snippets of her written work on the platform. She wrote her first ever book ," THE TEN STEPS" when she was just 15 , and did not release it until she was 16, in 2017. Urja joshi has three books published under her name, and are copyrighted to her. With the release of her poetry book in 2020 "YELLOW', She became the youngest bestselling author of India, and won many awards which made her "best poetry author 2021" and best female author 2020.her book "yellow" continued to be in the top 100 books of 2020 for whole 3 months after its release. she loves to experiment with her projects and she would love to write books from other genres as well. She wants to have her book tour one day, and she also wants to collaborate with many artists when it comes to song writing. She wants to be a young writer with a positive influence on her audience, and she also wishes for her poetry to reach people of different cultures, ethnicity and countries.

Urja joshi